101
fabulous Fat-Quarter Bags
with M'Liss Rae Hawley

C&T PUBLISHING

Text © 2008 by M'Liss Rae Hawley

Artwork © 2008 by C&T Publishing, Inc.

Publisher: Amy Marson

Creative Director: Gailen Runge

Acquisitions Editor: Jan Grigsby

Editor: Deb Rowden

Technical Editors: Sandy Peterson and Teresa Stroin

Copyeditor/Proofreader: Wordfirm Inc.

Cover and Book Designer: Kristy K. Zacharias

Illustrator: Tim Manibusan

Production Coordinators: Kirstie L. Pettersen, Matt Allen, and Kiera Lofgreen

Production Assistant: Casey Dukes

Photography: Luke Mulks and Diane Pedersen unless otherwise noted

Cover and Location Photography: Michael Stadler

Published by C&T Publishing, Inc., P.O. Box 1456, Lafayette, CA 94549

Library of Congress Cataloging-in-Publication Data

Hawley, M'Liss Rae
  101 fabulous fat-quarter bags with M'Liss Rae Hawley / M'Liss Rae Hawley.
    p. cm.
  Includes index.
  Summary: "A snappy, photo-rich, inspirational and how-to book featuring instructions for fat-quarter-friendly purses, small bags, totes, and small projects"—Provided by publisher.
  ISBN 978-1-57120-558-2 (paper trade : alk. paper)
  1. Handbags. 2. Patchwork—Patterns. 3. Fancy work. I. Title. II. Title: One hundred and one fabulous fat-quarter bags with M'Liss Rae Hawley.

TT667.H395 2008
646.4'8--dc22
                                        2008007231

Printed in China

10 9 8 7 6 5 4

Acknowledgments

I would like to thank the following people and companies who share my vision, enthusiasm, and love of quilting, and who contributed to the creation of this book.

C&T Publishing: Amy Marson, Jan Grigsby, Gailen Runge, Darra Williamson, Deb Rowden, Sandy Peterson, Kristy Zacharias, Kirstie L. Pettersen, Tim Manibusan, Matt Allen, Kiera Lofgreen, Casey Dukes, and all the staff who continue to create wonderful books.

Electric Quilt

Husqvarna Viking

Hoffman Fabrics

Jo-Ann Fabric and Craft Stores

Quilters Dream Batting

Robison-Anton Textiles

Alice

Michael Hawley

A special thank you to my contributors—an amazing group of dedicated and talented quilters. They continue to inspire me in many ways.

Contents

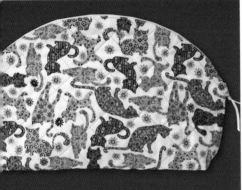

Dedication

To Adrienne Blythe Hawley, my daughter, best friend, and travel companion, I lovingly dedicate this book. She has packed "my bags" for travel all over the world, joining me on all my trips abroad and on many here in the States. Adrienne: muchas gracias, merci, danke, manga tak, tack så mycket, dzieki, köszönöm . . .

Introduction

Purses, tote bags, shopping bags—just think of the means we use in a single day to carry our most personal possessions. While it is possible to depend upon what the marketplace (or the grocery store!) has to offer, it's so easy, so rewarding—and *so much fun!*—to let our creativity take over and to make our own. Just flip through the pages of this book and you'll quickly see: the options for personal expression are endless!

My own love affair with purses, bags, and totes began when I was a little girl. To put it simply: I adored every one I saw! So great was my attraction that whenever my parents, family members, or friends traveled, my souvenir of choice was a purse.

As soon as I was able to stitch, I made bags to hold my baby dolls. When I graduated to Barbie dolls, they needed purses for each outfit . . . of course!

My enthusiasm was spurred even further by the new outfits I received for each special holiday: at Easter, an ensemble, complete with dress, coat, hat, gloves, shoes . . . and matching purse; at Christmas, a camel hair coat, red velvet dress . . . and matching purse with all the accessories.

Before long, the manufacturers could not keep pace with my imagination, so I began designing and making customized purses and totes to coordinate with the clothes I had started to make for myself. I searched for every possible fabric, fiber, and embellishment to personalize my creations. I tracked down resources for fur, leather, and everything shiny. I dyed, carded, and spun wool, and embroidered ribbon to weave into purses and bags. I knitted, crocheted, and used felted wool. I cut up and transformed my old blue jeans into stylish, sturdy totes. I even carved stamps with original patterns for a bag to match a favorite dress. As the years passed, my passion never faded. If anything, I became more inspired.

I love to travel—it is a big part of my "quilting" as well as my personal life—and over the years, my original purses, bags, and totes have accompanied me to all 50 states; throughout Canada; to northern, central, and eastern Europe; to South America; and to Asia. When I'm traveling, I'm always on the lookout for a source of inspiration or for a wonderful new fabric, fiber, or embellishment to adorn my next creation. You'll see the results in many of the examples in this book, including *Experience the World with M'Liss* (page 38), a fat-quarter tote bag made with fabric of the same name that I designed for Jo-Ann Fabric and Craft Stores.

I've had a great time designing and making the purses and tote bags in these pages. I hope you'll enjoy using them as a springboard for your own creativity.

Fabric Selection

Be creative in your fabric choices for these purses and totes. In addition to 100% quilter's cotton, the bags shown in this book feature the following:

- Damask and other tapestry-like fabrics
- Denim
- Dutch wax batiks and other ethnic fabrics
- Home-decorator cottons, blends, and weaves
- Leather and vinyl
- Organza, tulle netting, and other sheers
- Prequilted cotton
- Purchased panels and recycled fabrics
- Silks, including dupioni
- Ultrasuede
- Velvet
- Wool and felted wool

Fat Quarters

Look for symbols at the beginning of each purse project—they show how many fat quartes you need.

Interfacings and Stabilizers

These products come in many varieties (e.g., iron-on and water-soluble) and weights (including the heavier weights used for draperies) and are key ingredients in the construction of many of these purses and totes. They provide stabilization for machine embroidery and other embellishments and add structure and shape to the finished bag. I have made recommendations to guide you in the specific project instructions, but in making your final choice, consider the end use of the bag and the form and weight of any embellishments you are using.

General Sewing Tips

If your machine has such a feature, set the sewing advisor to heavy fabric to accommodate the weight of the fabrics (especially many specialty fabrics), battings, and interfacings.

Whenever possible, match the color of the top and bottom threads. I typically use 100% cotton thread for piecing.

Match the needle to the fabric and the job . . . and change the needle often! Many of these projects require a quilting needle; size 14 works well.

FAT-QUARTER CARRYALL p. 43

Projects

ORIGAMI BAG p. 24

CUBE PURSE p. 19

COSMETIC BAG p. 48

RIBBON PURSE p. 14

Small Shoulder Purse with Flap

FINISHED SIZE: approximately 7¼″ × 8½″

Evening Elegance. Designed and made by M'Liss Rae Hawley, 2007.

This is a quick and easy purse to sew, so you can make one for every special outfit, mood, holiday, or occasion. Because of its small size, it is a great opportunity to try a new embellishing technique, and its versatility makes it a great gift for a lady of any age . . . even the very youngest!

As you can see, I was inspired to make a wide variety of these little gems, and my quilting group was inspired, too. Altogether, you'll find more than 45 of them scattered throughout the pages of this book, each with something different to offer in terms of fabric choice, handle choice, and embellishment ideas.

Note: The working area of the flap—that is, the area visible on the *front* of the purse when the flap is closed—measures approximately 7″ wide by 6″ high. Keep this in mind when planning embellishing techniques and photo transfers.

Materials for the Basic Bag

A fat quarter assumes fabric that measures 17½″ × 20″ after laundering.

Bag flap: 1 fat quarter

Bag body: 1 fat quarter

Lining: 1 fat quarter

Medium to heavyweight iron-on stabilizer: ⅓ yard (40″ wide) or ⅝ yard (18″ wide)

Matching and/or contrasting threads for topstitching and/or quilting

Shoulder strap: Look at the beautiful photos in this chapter for handle ideas, or refer to Handle Ideas and How-Tos on page 51 for more suggestions and inspiration. Add the handle to the bag body after the flap is attached.

Cutting

Cut measurements include ¼″-wide seam allowances.

From the fat quarter for the flap:

Cut 1 piece, 7½″ × 8″.*

From the fat quarter for the body:

Cut 1 piece, 7¾″ × 17″.

From the fat quarter for the lining:

Cut 1 piece, 7½″ × 8″, for the flap lining.

Cut 1 piece, 7¾″ × 15″, for the body lining.

From the iron-on stabilizer:

Cut 1 piece, 7¼″ × 7¾″, for the flap lining.

Cut 1 piece, 7½″ × 14¾″, for the body lining.

*If you plan to embroider a motif on the flap, cut this piece a few inches larger in each direction to fit in your hoop and allow for shrinkage, and then trim the piece to size when the embroidery is complete.

Assembling the Purse

Use a ¼″ seam allowance for all seams.

1. Follow the manufacturer's instructions to iron the 7¼″ × 7¾″ piece of stabilizer to the wrong side of the 7½″ × 8″ piece of flap lining fabric, and iron the 7½″ × 14¾″ piece of stabilizer to the wrong side of the 7¾″ × 15″ piece of body lining fabric. Note: If you intend to embellish the flap, iron the stabilizer to the flap fabric instead of the flap lining fabric.

Reinforce It!

If you plan to add a heavy embellishment to your bag, add extra interfacing to the bag body and the flap as well.

---

2. If you plan to embellish the flap with machine embroidery, crazy patch work, fabric manipulation, or any other technique that would go through to the back of the flap, then now is the time. Refer to the photos throughout this chapter, and see Embellishment: Making It Yours (page 57) for inspiration. If you plan to add trims, beading, or buttons, etc., which don't significantly affect the back of the flap, then do this type of embellishment after Step 3.

3. Place the 7½″ × 8″ piece of stabilized flap lining fabric right sides together with the 7½″ × 8″ piece of flap fabric, and pin the layers together. Sew around the perimeter of the unit, leaving a 2″ opening at the top edge for turning. Clip the corners, and turn the flap right side out. Turn the raw edges of the opening inward, press the flap, and topstitch around the perimeter of the flap with matching or contrasting thread.

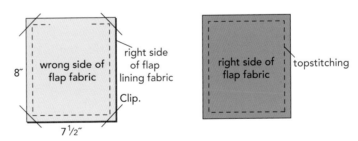

4. Fold the 7¾″ × 17″ piece of body fabric in half crosswise with right sides together, aligning the short raw edges. Press. Sew the 2 side seams, and press the seams open. Clip the corners as needed, and turn the body right side out. Turn the top raw edge of the bag ½″ to the wrong side and press.

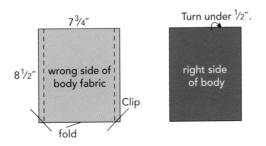

Two-Fabric Flap Option

Instead of cutting 1 piece, 7½" × 8", for the flap:

From the flap fabric:

Cut 1 piece, 7½" × 5".

From additional body fabric:

Cut 1 piece, 7½" × 3½".

Sew the 2 pieces right sides together along the 7½" edge, press the seam open, and proceed with Assembling the Purse, Step 1.

An Evening in Singapore. Designed and made by M'Liss Rae Hawley, 2007.

---

5. Repeat Step 4, folding and sewing the 7¾" × 15" piece of stabilized body lining fabric. *Do not turn the sewn body lining right side out.*

6. Insert the body lining from Step 5 inside the body from Step 4, and smooth to fit, matching the side seams. (The wrong side of the bag should face the interfaced side of the lining.) Turn the folded edge of the body over another ½" so it covers the raw edge of the lining. Press.

7. Using the walking or dual-feed foot attachment and the free arm on your sewing machine, topstitch the turned-over edge of the bag to the lining with matching or contrasting thread.

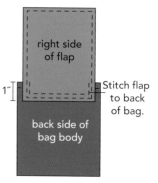

8. Place the lined bag body with the back faceup on your work surface. Center the lined flap unit with the right or front side up over the back of the bag so the bottom edge of the flap overlaps the back of the bag by approximately 1". (You may wish to draw a chalk line 1" from the back top edge of the bag for guidance in lining up the flap.) Using the free arm on your sewing machine, topstitch the flap to only the back of the bag, using matching or contrasting thread.

Clever Closure!

If you wish, make a buttonhole near the bottom center edge of the bag flap. Secure a decorative button to the bag body, and button the flap closed. If you prefer, you can make a loop from fabric or trim instead of a buttonhole.

ASYMMETRICAL FLAP
Made by Cheryl Gilman, 2007.

FABRIC MOTIF CUT FOR FLAP
Made by Susie Kincy, 2007.

ROUNDED FLAP
Made by Susie Kincy, 2007.

POINTED FLAP
Made by Lucia Pan, 2007.

Additional Flap Options

In addition to the two-fabric flap option, there are many other creative ways to shape the flap for this versatile purse. Here are just a few of the countless possibilities.

SCALLOPED FLAP
Made by Susie Kincy, 2007.

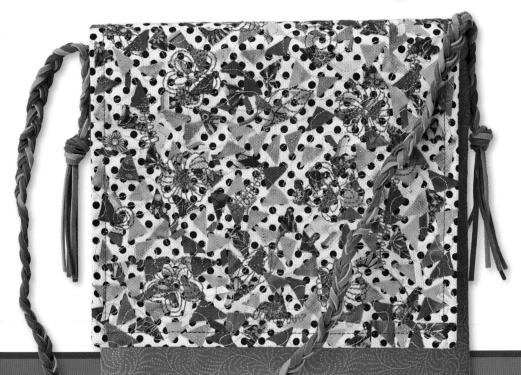

Petite Textures. Designed and made by M'Liss Rae Hawley, 2007.

Made by Susie Kincy, 2007.

Made by Barbara Dau, 2007.

Made by Louise James, 2007.

Made by Carla Zimmermann, 2007.

Meow! Designed and made by M'Liss Rae Hawley, 2007.

Made by Carla Zimmermann, 2007.

Wedding Memories. Designed and made by M'Liss Rae Hawley, 2007.

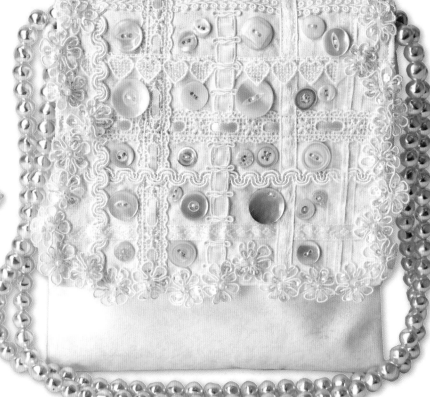

Made by Annette Barca, 2007.

Made by Annette Barca, 2007.

Made by Vicki DeGraaf, 2007.

Made by Vicki DeGraaf, 2007.

Made by Annette Barca, 2007.

Mardi Gras. Designed and made by M'Liss Rae Hawley, 2007.

Sunflower Designed and made by M'Liss Rae Hawley, 2007.

Made by Cheryl Gilman, 2007.

Made by Lucia Pan, 2007.

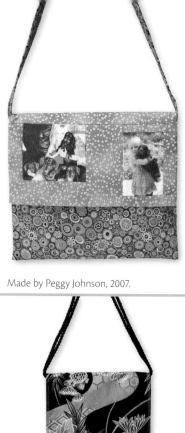

Made by Peggy Johnson, 2007.

Made by Lucia Pan, 2007.

Made by Cheryl Gilman, 2007.

Made by Susie Kincy, 2007.

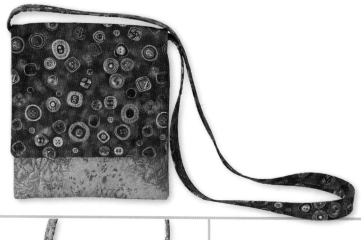

Made by John James, 2007.

Hello Kitty for Adrienne. Designed and made by M'Liss Rae Hawley, 2007.

Made by Clara Hagglund, 2007.

Made by Annette Barca, 2007.

Made by Susie Kincy, 2007.

Made by Susie Kincy, 2007.

Made by Cheryl Gilman, 2007.

Made by Cheryl Gilman, 2007.

Zippers! Designed and made by M'Liss Rae Hawley, 2007.

Made by Susie Kincy, 2007.

Made by Carla Zimmermann, 2007.

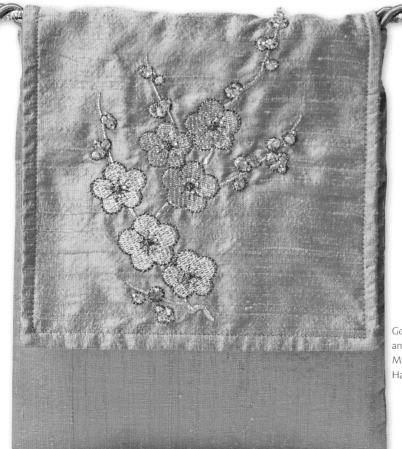

Gold. Designed and made by M'Liss Rae Hawley, 2007.

Made by Carla Zimmermann, 2007.

Small Shoulder Purse with Flap

Ribbon Purse

FINISHED SIZE: approximately 12″ × 10″

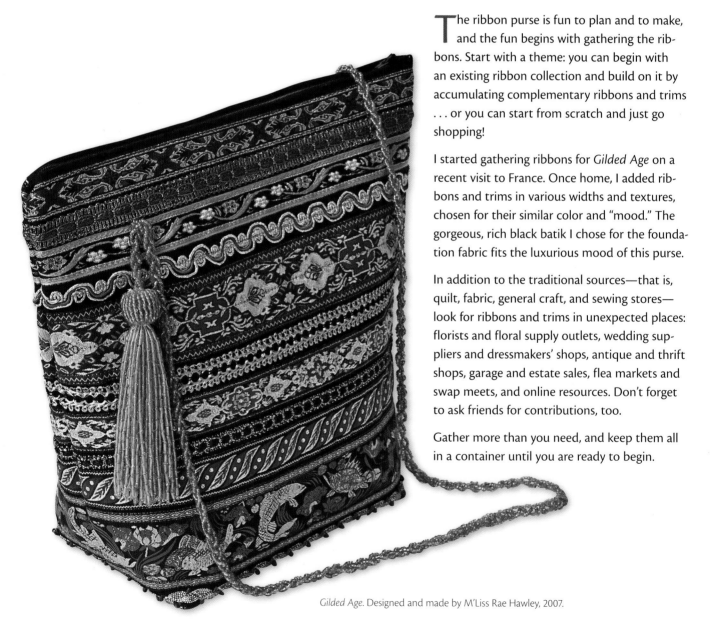

The ribbon purse is fun to plan and to make, and the fun begins with gathering the ribbons. Start with a theme: you can begin with an existing ribbon collection and build on it by accumulating complementary ribbons and trims . . . or you can start from scratch and just go shopping!

I started gathering ribbons for *Gilded Age* on a recent visit to France. Once home, I added ribbons and trims in various widths and textures, chosen for their similar color and "mood." The gorgeous, rich black batik I chose for the foundation fabric fits the luxurious mood of this purse.

In addition to the traditional sources—that is, quilt, fabric, general craft, and sewing stores— look for ribbons and trims in unexpected places: florists and floral supply outlets, wedding suppliers and dressmakers' shops, antique and thrift shops, garage and estate sales, flea markets and swap meets, and online resources. Don't forget to ask friends for contributions, too.

Gather more than you need, and keep them all in a container until you are ready to begin.

Gilded Age. Designed and made by M'Liss Rae Hawley, 2007.

Materials for the Basic Bag

A fat quarter assumes fabric that measures 17½" × 20" after laundering.

Bag foundation*: 2 fat quarters

Lining: 2 fat quarters

Ribbons and trims in assorted widths and textures: Lots of 13½" lengths in matching pairs

Handle: 3 yards of silk cord or braided strands of delicate beads

Tassels: 2 to match handle material

Heavyweight iron-on stabilizer: ½ yard (40" wide) or ⅞ yard (18" wide)

Matching and/or contrasting threads for topstitching the ribbons and trims

12" zipper

Chalk pencil or marker

Fray Check

Terry-cloth towel

Timtex or fast2fuse interfacing: 7½" × 4½" piece (optional)

* This fabric may or may not show depending on your design.

Cutting

From *each* fat quarter for the bag foundation:

Cut 1 piece, 13" × 14½" (2 total).

From *each* fat quarter for the lining:

Cut 1 piece, 13" × 14½" (2 total).

From the heavyweight iron-on stabilizer:

Cut 2 pieces, 12¾" × 14¼".

Preparing the Ribbon Panels

See Tips for Working with Ribbons and Trims (page 16) before you begin.

1. Follow the manufacturer's instructions to iron a 12¾" × 14¼" piece of stabilizer to the wrong side of each 13" × 14½" piece of bag foundation fabric.

2. Use a chalk pencil or marker to draw a line 1½" from the top raw edge and ½" from the bottom raw edge on the right (fabric) side of each 13" × 14½" stabilized bag foundation piece. You will not sew ribbon in these marked-off areas. The top line is a guideline for placing the zipper; the bottom line indicates the bottom seam.

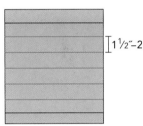

3. Mark lines approximately 1½" to 2" apart on the right (fabric) side in the same place on each stabilized bag foundation piece, keeping the lines between and parallel to the lines you marked in Step 2. These lines will be guidelines for keeping the ribbons and trims straight as you place them on the bag foundation fabric.

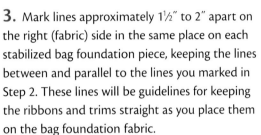

4. Sort the 13½" lengths of ribbons and trims into 2 identical stacks. Place 1 unit from Step 3, marked side up, on your design wall or other flat surface. Audition 1 stack of ribbons and trims for placement between the top and bottom marked lines. Occasionally step back and look through a reducing glass, or take a digital photo to observe the overall effect. **Note:** The area of the purse that shows after the bottom is squared ends approximately 2¼" from the bottom seam. Plan your placement of ribbons and trims accordingly.

5. Working 1 ribbon at a time, and using the mock-up you created in Step 4 as a guide, begin topstitching the same ribbons and trims from the *second* stack to the marked side of the *remaining* marked unit from Step 3, placing them in the same order. Check the ribbons and trims occasionally to be sure that they are straight; adjust as necessary.

topstitching

6. Using the stitched panel from Step 5 as a guide, topstitch the ribbons and trims to the unit from your design wall (Step 4). Measure and compare the placement of the ribbons as you go. The 2 stitched panels must be identical for the ribbons and trims to match exactly when the panels are sewn together.

7. Staystitch with a *scant* ¼″ seam around the perimeter of each panel. Square up the edges of each panel, trimming any excess ribbon and/or trim. Apply Fray Check to the cut edges to prevent raveling.

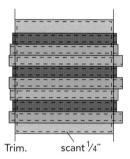

Trim.   scant ¼″

Assembling the Purse

1. With right sides together, and beginning with a regular stitch for the first ½″, machine baste the 2 ribbon panels together ¼″ from the top edge of the uppermost ribbon. End with a regular stitch length for the last ½″. Place the unit on a terry-cloth towel and carefully press the seam open.

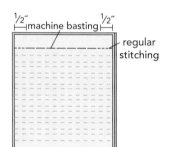

½″ |machine basting| ½″

regular stitching

2. Working with the zipper tape on top, place the zipper teeth against the basted seam from Step 1, and sew the zipper into the top of the bag. Remove the basting stitches.

Open Wide!

Unzip the zipper before you sew the side and bottom seams of the bag.

Tips for Working with Ribbons and Trims

- Look for a thread that blends with the colors of all your ribbons and trims. I used Robison-Anton #1007, Antique Gold (see Resources on page 63). It's a black-and-gold twist that looked great with all my ribbons. On the other hand, Susie Kincy matched the thread to each ribbon and trim, and the results are wonderful.

- Some ribbons and trims may require more than topstitching on the outer edges. Add a second row of stitching ¼″ inside the first, or stitch down the center of the ribbon or trim.

- If you use a ribbon or trim that is dimensional, or is loosely woven or loopy, you may want to add extra stitching to prevent snagging.

- Place the ribbons so that they touch, or space them slightly apart to show glimpses of the foundation fabric. Cheryl Gilman used fewer ribbons and trims and spaced them so lots of background shows to become part of the overall effect.

Cheryl left lots of space between the ribbons and trims on her purse. Notice her use of torn denim for some of the strips. For a full view, see page 18.

3. With right sides of the panels together, pin and sew the side seams using a ¼″ seam allowance, carefully matching the ends of the ribbons and trims. Sew the bottom seam using the ½″ seam allowance, stitching right along the edges of the bottommost ribbons. Serge or zigzag the side seams and the bottom seam to finish.

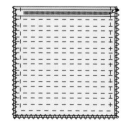

4. Fold the bag—still right sides together—so 1 long side seam runs down the center, facing you. (The bag will form a large triangle.) Measure 2¼" from the tip; mark, and stitch across the point as shown to form a gusset. Repeat on the other side seam. Turn the bag right side out. If desired, place a 7½" × 4½" piece of Timtex or fast2fuse interfacing in the bottom of the purse.

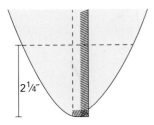

2¼"

5. Hand stitch the 3 yards of silk cord or the braided beads to the outside of the purse, placing the ends (and a tassel) on opposite sides of the 2 outside panels, and trimming the length if necessary. If you prefer a different handle treatment, refer to Handle Ideas and How-Tos (page 51) for other options.

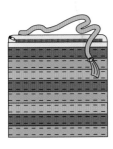

(page 51)

Add a Label Now

If you want to add a label to your purse lining, now is a good time to do that. It's harder to do that later, after it's assembled.

Assembling and Inserting the Lining

1. With right sides together, sew the 13" × 14½" rectangles of lining fabric together along the side and the bottom edges using a ¼" seam allowance. Serge or zigzag the seams to finish.

2. Finish the bottom edge of the lining as described in Assembling the Purse, Step 4. *Do not turn the lining right side out.*

3. Insert the lining from Step 2 inside the bag body and smooth to fit, matching the side seams. (The wrong side of the bag should face the wrong side of the lining.) Fold under the top edge of the lining so it aligns with the edge of the zipper and hand stitch in place along the machine stitching line.

Be sure to leave enough room for the zipper to open and close easily.

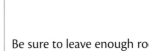
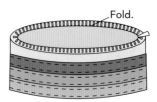

Fold.

Place a Pocket!

If you want to add a small pocket to the lining of your bag, you'll need to do it before the lining is inserted in the bag.

Cut 2 squares of lining fabric 4½" × 4½". Place them right sides together with raw edges aligned, and stitch around the perimeter with a ¼" seam allowance, leaving a 1½" opening along 1 side for turning. Clip the corners, and turn the unit right side out. Turn the raw edges of the opening inward, press, and topstitch around the perimeter with matching thread. Place the pocket, and stitch around 3 sides to secure it to the lining.

Made by Susie Kincy, 2007.

Made by Cheryl Gilman, 2007.

Made by Cheryl Gilman, 2007.

Made by Barbara Dau, 2007.

Made by Cheryl Gilman, 2007.

Made by Clara Hagglund, 2007.

The Cube Purse

FINISHED SIZE: approximately 8″ × 8″

The shape of this purse was inspired by a simple straw bag—I made some modifications in design and construction to convert it to fabric (fat quarters from my collection, *M'Liss's Garden*, of course!), upgraded it with handsome wooden handles, and edged it with prairie points for added interest and style. The result is a bag so versatile and roomy that you can use it as a casual purse or a small tote . . . perfect for carrying a small book and a snack to the park or for bringing home small purchases from your morning errands.

The Cube. Designed and made by M'Liss Rae Hawley, 2007.

Materials for the Basic Bag

A fat quarter assumes fabric that measures 17½" × 20" after laundering.

Outer bag and prairie-point trim:
4 fat quarters

Lining and prairie-point trim:
2 fat quarters

Medium to heavyweight iron-on stabilizer: ⅞ yard (40" wide) or 1¼ yards (18" wide)

Batting: 4 squares 8" × 8"

fast2fuse interfacing: 2 squares 8" × 8"

Purchased half-round wooden handles: 2; approximately 7" diameter each

Matching and/or contrasting threads for topstitching and/or quilting

Fabric spray adhesive

Pinking shears

Fabric glue (optional)

Cutting

Cut measurements include ¼"-wide seam allowances.

From *each* fat quarter of outer-bag fabric:

Cut 2 pieces, 4¾" × 8½" (8 total).

From 1 fat quarter of outer-bag fabric:

Cut 1 square, 8½" × 8½", for the bag bottom.

From a different fat quarter of outer-bag fabric:

Cut 1 strip, 3⅛" × 18", for the handle tabs.

From 1 fat quarter of lining fabric:

Cut 4 squares, 8½" × 8½", for the sides.

From the second fat quarter of lining fabric:

Cut 3 squares, 8½" × 8½", for the bottom.

From the assorted fat quarters of outer-bag and lining fabric:

Cut *a total of* 24 squares, 3½" × 3½", in matching pairs for the prairie-point trim.

From the iron-on stabilizer:

Cut 10 squares, 8⅜" × 8⅜".

Assembling the Outer Bag

Use a ¼" seam allowance for all seams.

1. With right sides together, sew 2 different 4¾" × 8½" rectangles of outer-bag fabric together along their long edges. Press the seams to one side. Make 2 identical units.

2. Repeat Step 1 using the remaining 4¾" × 8½" rectangles of outer-bag fabric. You will have a total of 4 units in 2 identical pairs, each measuring 9" × 8½".

 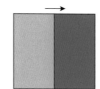

Make 2 each.

3. Follow the manufacturer's instructions to center and iron an 8⅜" square of stabilizer on the wrong side of each unit from Step 2. Repeat using an 8⅜" square of stabilizer and the 8½" square of outer-bag fabric for the bottom of the bag. Set this piece aside.

Made by Cheryl Gilman, 2007.

4. Use fabric spray adhesive to center and adhere an 8″ square of batting over the stabilizer on each 9″ × 8½″ unit from Step 3. Machine quilt as desired.

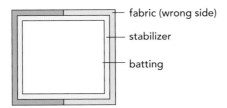

fabric (wrong side)

stabilizer

batting

5. Measure and mark 4¼″ in each direction from the center seam of each unit from Step 4. Trim. The unit should now measure 8½″ × 8½″.

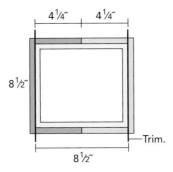

4¼″ 4¼″

8½″

Trim.

8½″

6. Arrange the units from Step 5, fabric side up, alternating them as shown. With right sides together, sew the units together. Press the seams to one side. Trim the top edge so the new unit measures 8¼″ high. This raw edge of the stabilized fabric will now be even with the batting; this will be the top edge of the bag.

Trim.

8¼″

7. Fold the unit from Step 6 right sides together, aligning the 2 short raw edges that are 8¼″ high. Sew along the short raw edges.

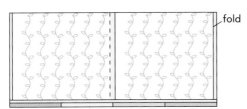

fold

8. Open the unit into a box. It will have a seam in each corner and matching panels on opposite sides.

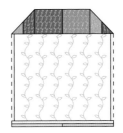

9. With right sides together, align the corners of the bottom 8½″ square of stabilized fabric from Step 3 with the corner seams of the box unit from Step 8. Sew the bottom square into the box using a ¼″ seam. Set aside.

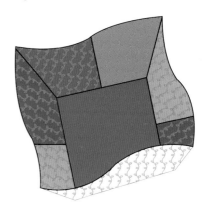

10. Follow the manufacturer's instructions to center and adhere the 8″ squares of fast2fuse interfacing to the wrong side of two 8½″ squares of bottom lining fabric. With fast2fuse sides together, adhere the fabric squares together. Trim using pinking shears, and serge or use a zigzag stitch to finish the square to 8″.

11. Turn the outer bag from Step 9 right side out and insert the square from Step 10 into the bag bottom. Secure with fabric glue if desired.

Assembling and Inserting the Lining

1. Follow the manufacturer's instructions to center and iron an 8⅜" square of stabilizer to the wrong side of each of the 4 matching 8½" squares of lining fabric for the sides and the remaining 8½" square of lining fabric for the bag bottom.

Plan Ahead!

If you plan to sew a label into your bag, now is the time! Place it as you wish on the fabric side of 1 stabilized lining square—making sure to leave ample room for trimming and seam allowances—and stitch the label in place.

---

2. With right sides together, sew the 4 matching units from Step 1 together. Press the seams to one side. Refer to Assembling the Outer Bag, Steps 7 and 8, to assemble the lining unit into a box and to insert the 8½" bottom square.

3. Insert the lining from Step 2 into the outer bag on top of the fast2fuse square and smooth to fit, matching the corner seams. (The wrong side of the bag should face the stabilized side of the lining.) Machine baste along the top edge to secure the layers.

Adding the Handle and Finishing

1. Place 2 matching 3½" squares of outer-bag or lining fabric right sides together. Sew all around the perimeter of the square. Clip the corners (and trim the seam allowance with pinking shears if necessary to reduce bulk), and make a slit in 1 side of the square unit, being careful not to cut through to the facing square. Turn the square right side out, smooth and square the corners, press, and topstitch around the edges.

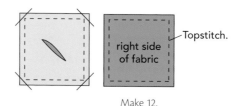

Make 12.

Made by Susie Kincy, 2007.

2. Fold and evenly space the squares from Step 1 over the raw top edge of the bag, overlapping the squares approximately 1½″ and mixing the colors for visual appeal. Sew the squares to the bag with decorative stitching.

3. Fold the 3⅛″ × 18″ strip of outer-bag fabric in half lengthwise, right sides together and with raw edges aligned. Sew the long, 18″ edge, and press the seam open. Turn the unit right side out, and cut it into 4 segments, each 4½″ long.

To Turn Tubes

Try products like the Fasturn or other tube turners. They help turn long, narrow tubes of fabric right side out easily.

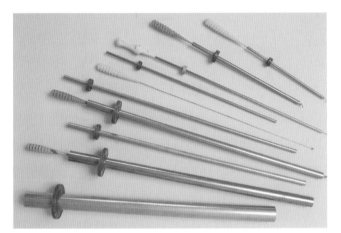

The Fasturn, available at many quilt, fabric, and craft stores

4. Measure the diameter of the handle and mark the bag for handle placement. Place 1 of the tabs from Step 3 through each loop of one handle, fold each tab in half, turn the raw edges under, pin, and stitch. Position the tabs inside the bag, and stitch them in place, using the same decorative stitch used to attach the prairie-point trim. If you wish, add additional securing stitches by hand. Attach the second handle the same way on the opposite side of the bag.

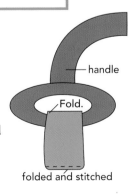

handle

Fold.

folded and stitched

Origami Bag

FINISHED SIZE: approximately 6″ × 6″

I love this little bag, which is created by folding fabric much as you would fold paper to make a traditional origami piece. The size, shape, and style make it ideal to use as an evening bag, but it could also work for packing jewelry, cosmetics, or other small items for travel. You may just want to display this on your coffee table—it's so pretty and sculptural . . .

Four Continents. Designed and made by M'Liss Rae Hawley, 2007.

Materials for the Basic Bag

A fat quarter assumes fabric that measures 17½″ × 20″ after laundering.

Outer bag: 1 fat quarter

Outer-bag accent: 1 fat quarter

Lining: 1 fat quarter

Flannel or diaper flannel: 17″ × 17″ square

Matching and/or contrasting threads for topstitching and/or quilting

Ribbon: 1½ yards *each* of ⅛″-wide ribbon in 2 contrasting colors for the handle/closure

Silk cord: 1½ yards to match 1 ribbon color for the handle/closure

Decorative rings: 4 wood or metal; ¾″ diameter

Cutting

Cut measurements include ¼″-wide seam allowances.

From the outer-bag fabric:

Cut 1 square, 12″ × 12″.

From the outer-bag accent fabric:

Cut 2 strips, 3″ × 12″, for the top and bottom accent borders.

Cut 2 strips, 3″ × 17″, for the side accent borders.

From the lining fabric:

Cut 1 square, 17″ × 17″.

Assembling the Bag

Use a ¼″ seam allowance for all seams.

1. Sew 3″ × 12″ outer-bag accent strips to the top and bottom of the 12″ square of outer-bag fabric. Press toward the border. Sew the 3″ × 17″ outer-bag accent strips to the sides. Press toward the border.

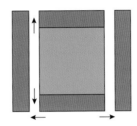

2. Place the 17″ square of lining fabric and the unit from Step 1 right sides together. Layer the 17″ square of flannel on top. Sew around the perimeter, leaving a 4″ opening on 1 side for turning. Clip the corners, turn the unit right side out, and slipstitch the opening closed.

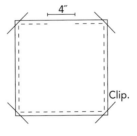

3. Topstitch around the perimeter of the bag approximately ⅛″ from the finished edges. Machine quilt as desired.

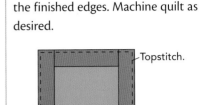

Topstitch.

4. Place the bag—lining up—on your work surface. Bring each corner in to meet at the top of the bag. Hand stitch along the 4½″ section shown on all 4 edges to make 4 flaps.

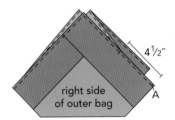

4½″

right side of outer bag

A

5. Turn the flap inside out by pushing Point A (located on the outer edge of the hand-stitched seam) into the interior of the bag to make

Made by Susie Kincy, 2007.

a 2-layered triangular flap with its right sides together. Repeat on remaining 3 flaps.

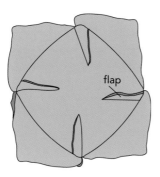

6. Turn the bag lining side out, shaping it so the bottom lies flat and the pleated flaps stand out from each corner. Working 1 corner at a time, turn the flap to the right, and pin it to the lining. Use matching thread to carefully hand stitch the flap to the lining, taking care not to stitch through to the front of the bag. Repeat for each flap. Turn the bag right side out, and shape.

Finishing the Bag

1. Hand stitch a ¾" decorative ring to the lining just inside the edge of each corner of the bag.

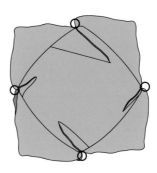

2. Cut each ribbon and the silk cording into 2 pieces of equal length. Arrange a length of each color ribbon and a length of cording side by side, and tie them together at both ends. Make 2.

3. Weave a tied length of ribbon/cording through rings 1, 2, and 3; tie the ends together. Weave a second length of ribbon/cording through rings 1, 4, and 3; tie the ends together.

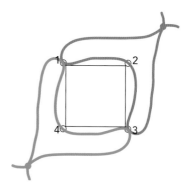

Made by John and Louise James, 2007.

Saddle Bag Purse

FINISHED SIZE: approximately 12½″ × 18″

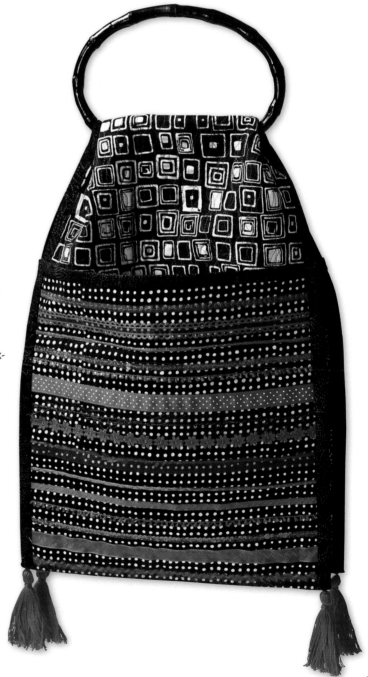

No doubt you'll receive lots of compliments when you carry this unusual and fun-to-make purse.

As is typical for me, I decided to "reduce my variables" in planning this purse. I began with a monochromatic color story of black-and-white batiks. I embellished them with an assortment of beautiful trims—all red—that I attached artfully with a variety of exciting techniques. Finally, I added red tassels that I made myself with cotton embroidery floss, and I purchased a black bamboo handle to continue the monochromatic color scheme.

Note: The working area of the pocket measures approximately 12″ square. Keep this in mind when planning embellishing techniques.

Along the Andes. Designed and made by M'Liss Rae Hawley, 2007.

Materials for the Basic Bag

Unless noted otherwise, yardages are based on fabric that measures 42" wide after laundering.

A fat quarter assumes fabric that measures 17½" × 20" after laundering.

Note: Handle your fat quarters carefully. Press them thoroughly, using spray starch. The size given above for a fat quarter is a conservative one. Many fat quarters will be large enough to cut the slightly larger pieces required for this bag.

Bag body (front): 3 fat quarters*, **

Bag pockets: 2 fat quarters**

Bag backing: 2 fat quarters**

Binding: ½ yard

Medium or heavyweight iron-on stabilizer: ½ yard (40" wide) or ⅞ yard (18" wide)

Thin batting or diaper flannel: 12½" × 60½" piece (after washing)

Matching and/or contrasting threads for topstitching and/or quilting

Decorative threads, ribbons, cording, and yarns for couching (optional)

Embroidery floss: 4 packages for tassels or 4 purchased tassels in coordinating colors

Purchased round lacquered handle: 7" diameter

Requires 12½" × 20½" pieces. See note above.

**May be the same or different fabrics.*

Cutting

Cut measurements include ¼"-wide seam allowances.

From *each* fat quarter for the bag pockets:

Cut 1 square, 13" × 13" (2 total).

From *each* fat quarter for the bag backing:

Cut 1 piece, 12½" × 18½" (2 total).

From *each* fat quarter for the bag body (front):

Cut 1 piece, 12½" × 20½" (3 total).

From the iron-on stabilizer:

Cut 2 pieces, 12⅞" × 12⅞", for the pockets.

From the binding fabric:

Cut 4 strips, 3" × 42".

Assembling the Purse

Use a ¼" seam allowance for all seams.

1. Follow the manufacturer's instructions to iron a 12⅞" square of interfacing to the wrong side of each 13" pocket square.

2. If desired, embellish the fabric side of each pocket square with couching, using decorative threads, ribbons, cording, yarns, and so on. Refer to Embellishment: Making It Yours (page 57) and the many beautiful photos throughout this chapter for guidance and additional inspiration. Trim each pocket to measure 12½" square.

3. With right sides together, sew both 12½" × 18½" pieces of bag backing fabric together along 1 short side. The fat quarters that you use for the bag backing may be the same or different. Press. With right sides together, sew a pocket square unit to each of the opposite short ends of the unit, taking care to orient any embellishment as desired. Note that the arrows on the illustration point toward the edge of the pocket opening after purse assembling is complete. Press. If desired, couch a length of trim over the seams joining the pockets to the backing.

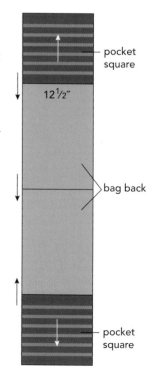

pocket square

12½"

bag back

pocket square

4. With right sides together, sew the three 12½″ × 20½″ pieces of bag body (front) fabric together along their short sides. The fat quarters that you use for the bag body front may be the same or different. Press.

Finishing the Purse

Refer to Embellishment Options and Fantastic Finishes (page 57) as needed.

1. Layer the bag body (front) wrong side up, the batting, and the bag backing (with pockets) right side up; baste.

2. Machine quilt as desired.

3. Use the 3″-wide strips to bind all the edges. I always use the same method. For instructions, see my *Round Robin Renaissance* book (C&T Publishing, 2006), pages 72–74.

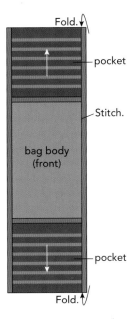

12½″

bag body (front)

Made by Lucia Pan, 2007.

4. Fold the pocket squares to the front of the bag, and machine stitch in the ditch along the binding on the sides of the pockets, or use a hand whipstitch or buttonhole/blanket stitch along the edges to join the sides of the pocket squares to the body of the bag to create pockets.

Fold.
pocket
Stitch.
bag body (front)
pocket
Fold.

5. Place the bag through the round handle so the ends of the bag are even and the pockets are on the outside. If you wish, hand stitch approximately ½″ of the binding together below the handle to keep the handle from slipping.

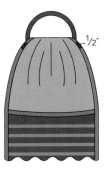

½″

6. Refer to Tassels (pages 61–62), and use 1 package of embroidery floss to make a tassel. Make 4, and hand stitch 1 to each of the bottom corners of each pocket.

Made by Annette Barca, 2007.

Made by Cheryl Gilman, 2007.

Made by Vicki DeGraaf, 2007.

Made by Peggy Johnson, 2007.

Made by Carla Zimmermann, 2007.

Made by John and Louise James, 2007.

Mix & Match Tote Bag

FINISHED SIZE: approximately 16″ × 17″

Just about every quilter has a collection of blocks that—for whatever reason—never made it into a quilt. Perhaps these blocks are leftovers from a finished project, blocks that you won at your quilt guild drawing or raffle, odd blocks you picked up at a garage or estate sale, or blocks gifted to you by a friend (or friends). Perhaps they are embroideries that you used for testing thread colors, or extras you made "just in case." If so, this versatile bag is for you!

The Mix & Match Tote allows you to use four 6″ blocks or one 12″ block—either from your existing collection or brand-new ones made just for this purpose.

For my tote, I used a couple of 6″ blocks from the block pool in my book *Mariner's Medallion Quilts* (C&T Publishing, 2006). As complements, I designed a Dog House block, which I made up in Ultrasuede, and a fourth block made by combining motifs from one of my embroidery collections (see Embroidery Collections on page 63). I added loads of fun embellishments to the basic bag to enhance the theme. You can make your tote as simple or as elaborate as you wish.

North by Northwest. Designed and made by M'Liss Rae Hawley, 2007.

Materials for the Basic Bag

Unless noted otherwise, yardages are based on fabric that measures 42" wide after laundering.

A fat quarter assumes fabric that measures 17½" × 20" after laundering.

Note: Handle your fat quarters carefully. Press them thoroughly, using spray starch. The size given above for a fat quarter is a conservative one. Many fat quarters will be large enough to cut the slightly larger pieces required for the handles of this bag.

Bag front (outer borders) and handles: 2 fat quarters*

Bag back and handles: 2 fat quarters*

Lining: 2 fat quarters

Inner border: 1 fat quarter

Four 6½" blocks (or one 12½" block) for front center "panel"*

Diaper flannel: ⅝ yard

Plain cording for handle: 4 yards; ½" diameter**

Decorative cording for handle: 2 yards; ½" diameter**

Fasturn tool (see page 23)**

Matching and/or contrasting thread for machine quilting and topstitching

* If you prefer a different handle than the one shown on page 34, you may need only 1 fat quarter of this fabric.

** If you prefer a different handle than the one shown on page 34, you may not need these items.

*** The 6½" blocks will finish to 6", the 12½" blocks will finish to 12".

Optional pocket: 2 fat quarters

Medium or heavyweight iron-on stabilizer for optional pocket: ½ yard (18" wide or 40" wide)

Cutting

Cut measurements include ¼"-wide seam allowances.

From the fat quarters for the bag back and handles:

Cut 1 piece, 17½" × 20", for the bag back.

Cut 4 strips, 2¼" × 21", for the handles.

From the fat quarters for the bag front (outer borders) and handles:

Cut 1 strip, 1½" × 14½", for the top outer border.

Cut 1 strip, 5" × 14½", for the bottom outer border.

Cut 2 strips, 2" × 20", for the side outer borders.

Cut 4 strips, 2¼" × 21", for the handles.

From the inner-border fabric:

Cut 2 pieces, 1½" × 12½", for the top and bottom.

Cut 2 pieces, 1½" × 14½", for the sides.

From each fat quarter for the lining:

Cut 1 piece, 17½" × 20" (2 total).

From the diaper flannel:

Cut 2 pieces, 17½" × 20".

Made by Annette Barca, 2007.

Assembling the Front Panel

Use a ¼″ seam allowance for all seams.

Note: If you are using a 12½″ block rather than four 6½″ blocks for the center panel, skip to Step 2.

1. Arrange the four 6½″ blocks in 2 horizontal rows of 2 blocks each. Sew the blocks together into rows. Press the seams in alternating directions from row to row. Sew the rows together to complete the center panel. Press.

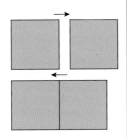

2. Sew 1½″ × 12½″ inner-border strips to the top and bottom of the center panel as shown in the diagram following Step 3. Press the seams toward the border. Sew the 1½″ × 14½″ inner-border strips to the sides. Press.

3. Sew the 1½″ × 14½″ outer-border strip to the top and the 5″ × 14½″ outer-border strip to the bottom of the unit from Step 2. Press the seams toward the newly added border. Sew the 2″ × 20″ outer-border strips to the sides. Press.

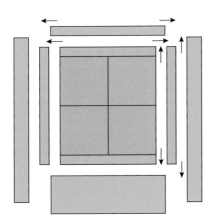

Place a Pocket

For extra carrying power, you might like to place a large pocket on the back of your tote. You will need 2 additional fat quarters—each cut into 1 piece 15½″ × 17½″ (for the front of the pocket and for the pocket lining)—and 1 piece 15¼″ × 17¼″ of iron-on stabilizer.

1. Following the manufacturer's instructions, center and iron the 15¼″ × 17¼″ piece of stabilizer to the wrong side of the 15½″ × 17½″ piece of pocket-front fabric. Place the stabilized fabric right sides together with the 15½″ × 17½″ piece of pocket lining, and stitch along the top edge with a ¼″ seam.

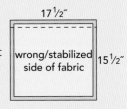

2. Open the unit from Step 1, and place the wrong sides together, folding along the seamline. Press. Topstitch ¼″ from the seamed top edge. Machine quilt as desired.

3. Baste the pocket, right side up, to the right side of the bag back, aligning the side and bottom raw edges. Proceed to assemble the bag as described below.

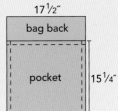

4. Center the unit from Step 3 right side up over a 17½″ × 20″ piece of diaper flannel; baste. Machine quilt as desired. Repeat, using the 17½″ × 20″ piece of fabric for the back of the bag and the remaining piece of diaper flannel.

Just for fun, I added lots of whimsical embellishment to the center panel of my tote *North by Northwest* (page 31). Use recycled jewelry—look for beads, buttons, charms, appliqués, threads, and trims that reflect your theme.

Assembling the Bag

1. Place the bag front and the bag back with right sides together, aligning the raw edges. Stitch around the side and bottom edges, leaving the top edge open.

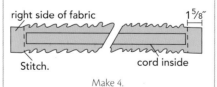

2. Fold the tote—still wrong side out—so 1 long side seam runs down the center, facing you. (The tote will form a large triangle.) Measure 3″ from the tip; mark, and stitch across the point to form a gusset. Repeat on the other side seam. Turn the tote right side out.

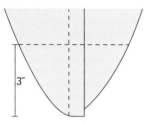

3″

3. Repeat Steps 1 and 2 using the two 17½″ × 20″ pieces of lining fabric to make the lining. *Do not turn the lining right side out.*

4. Insert the lining from Step 3 inside the bag body and smooth to fit, matching the seams and aligning the top raw edges. (The wrong side of the bag should face the wrong side of the lining.) Turn the top raw edges on both the bag and the lining ½″ to their wrong sides, press, and pin them together. Set the bag aside.

Making and Adding the Handles

The handles for the basic bag are braided using fabric-covered cords and complementary decorative cording. If you prefer a different handle treatment, refer to Handle Ideas and How-Tos (page 51) for other options.

1. Sew 2 strips 2¼″ × 21″ of bag-back fabric right sides together at right angles with a diagonal seam. Trim the seam allowance to ¼″, and press the seam open. (Refer to the photo on page 55 of Folded and Stitched do-it-yourself handles.) Make 2. Repeat using the 2¼″ × 21″ strips of bag-front fabric.

2. Fold a strip from Step 1 in half lengthwise, right sides together and with raw edges aligned. Sew the long raw edge, and press the seam open. Use a Fasturn tool to turn the unit right side out, and insert a 36″-long piece of plain ½″ cording into the tube. Make 4.

3. Determine the desired length of the handle (remember: braiding will affect the length), and scrunch the fabric up on the cording, leaving approximately 1⅝″ of scrunched fabric free of cording on both ends; stitch to secure. Repeat for all tubes.

right side of fabric   1⅝″

Stitch.   cord inside

Make 4.

4. To make each handle, braid 1 scrunched tube of each fabric with a 36″ length of decorative cording.

5. Place a pin to mark the center top edge of the bag front. Insert the unstuffed ends of 1 handle between the folded edge of the bag and the folded edge of the lining, approximately 4″ from either side of the marked center; pin. Repeat to insert and pin the remaining handle to the back of the bag.

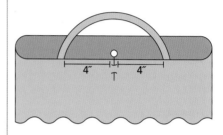

4″   T   4″

Insert a Closure

If you wish, insert any decorative closures between the turned hems of the bag and lining.

6. Topstitch all around the top edge of the bag to attach the lining and to secure the handles. Be sure to catch the unstuffed ends of both scrunched tubes and the ends of the decorative cording in the topstitching.

Made by John James, 2007.

Made by Lucia Pan, 2007.

Made by Clara Hagglund, 2007.

Made by Susie Kincy, 2007.

Panel Tote Bag

FINISHED SIZE: Will vary with size of panel

I purchased two beautiful dragon batik panels at our local quilt shop. It was one of those moments we all have where I thought, "I like them; what am I going to do with them?" Well, I always think of something! I call these my *'Treasures in Waiting'*! My advice: if you like something, buy it—or two! I love the Twin Dragons tote. The black batik around the edges really pops the design. The machine quilting adds great movement and dimension. Another "what am I going to do with these?" moments: I purchased the red leather handles in France, before I knew I was writing this book!

Twin Dragons. Designed and made by M'Liss Rae Hawley, 2007.

This panel tote is made from a home dec panel showing different professions in France. The piece of fabric I had was exactly the right size for the bag. Some of my *Spring Bouquet* fabrics blended beautifully, and continued the theme in the bag bottom, top band, lining, and handle. I machine quilted around each scene.

Here's a terrific way to put those fabulous panels or "too-pretty-to-cut" fabrics to use!

I would like to suggest my storage system of plastic containers to hold our *Treasures in Waiting!*

All in a Day's Work. Designed and made by M'Liss Rae Hawley, 2007.

Materials for the Basic Bag

A fat quarter assumes fabric that measures 17½″ × 20″ after laundering.

Outer bag: 2 equally sized panels, squares, or rectangles of fabric (2 fat quarters of the same fabric)

Accent border: 4 strips, 1½″ × width of outer-bag fabric (i.e., panel), and 4 strips, 1½″ × length of bag-body fabric plus 2″ (1 fat quarter)

Lining: 2 pieces of fabric equal to size of outer-body fabric, plus 2″ in both directions (2 fat quarters, or buy yardage if the lining dimensions would exceed the size of a fat quarter)

Batting or diaper flannel: 2 pieces equal to size of lining pieces

Handle: purchased (see Handle Ideas and How-Tos on page 51)

Matching and/or contrasting threads for topstitching and/or quilting

Assembling the Tote

Use a ¼″ seam allowance for all seams.

1. With right sides together, sew 1½″-wide accent strips to the top and bottom of an outer-bag panel, matching the length of the strip with the width of the outer-bag panel. Press the seams toward the accent strips. Sew the remaining 1½″-wide accent strips to the sides. Press. Repeat using the remaining panel and remaining 1½″-wide strips.

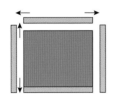

2. Layer a lining piece wrong side up, a piece of batting, and a unit from Step 1 right side up; baste. Repeat with the remaining unit from Step 1 and the remaining pieces of lining and batting. Quilt the panel areas as desired. Quilt in the ditch around the accent borders and ¼″ inside the accent border seam. Leave the balance of the accent border area free from quilting.

3. Place the 2 quilted units from Step 2 right sides (of the outer-bag panels) together, aligning the raw edges. Stitch around the side and bottom edges, leaving the top edge open. Serge or otherwise finish the seams and the top raw edge.

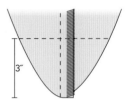

lined side of panel

stitched seam

serging

4. Fold the tote—still lining side out—so 1 long side seam runs down the center, facing you. (The tote will form a large triangle.) Measure 3″ from the tip; mark, and stitch across the point to form a gusset. Repeat on the other side seam. Turn the tote right side out.

3″

5. Fold the top accent border ½″ to the inside of the tote, and topstitch in place with 2 rows of stitches.

Fold. ½″

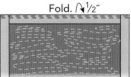

6. Refer to Handle Ideas and How-Tos (page 51), and attach the handles you've chosen to the front and the back of the tote.

Tip for Storing Treasures in Waiting

When you arrive home with treasures, the ones you bought, "just because," have a system in place for storage that uses prior, proper planning! I have see-through, plastic containers with lids. They are stacked on shelves, and each one is dedicated to specific products.

Made by John James, 2007.

Fat-Quarter Tote Bag

FINISHED SIZE: approximately 18½" × 21¼"

The Fat-Quarter Tote Bag offers creative opportunities that include machine embroidery, buttons, tassels, and prairie points, yet it goes together so easily that you can make one up quickly to give as a last-minute gift. I made two versions for this book. *Garden Court Winery* includes my original *Kimono Art* fabric and embroidery collections (Alice's favorite bag!). *Experience the World with M'Liss* (below) was made to showcase my new fabric line of the same name. This bag is perfect for tucking into your suitcase to bring home those souvenirs!

Garden Court Winery. Designed and made by M'Liss Rae Hawley, 2007.

Experience the World with M'Liss. Designed and made by M'Liss Rae Hawley, 2007.

Materials for the Basic Bag

Unless noted otherwise, yardages are based on fabric that measures 42" wide after laundering.

A fat quarter assumes fabric that measures 17½" × 20" after laundering.

Bag body and handle: 6 assorted fat quarters

Lining: 1⅜ yards

Thin batting or diaper flannel: 1⅜ yards

Decorative buttons: 2

Matching and/or contrasting threads for machine topstitching and/or quilting

Decorative thread for handle (optional)

Medium to heavyweight iron-on stabilizer: ¼ yard (40" wide)

Embroidery floss: 2 packages for tassels *or* 2 purchased tassels in coordinating colors

Cutting

Cut measurements include ¼"-wide seam allowances.

From 1 fat quarter:

Cut 1 rectangle, 12" × 19½", for the bag bottom (A).*, **

Cut 2 strips, 2" × 19½", for the upper bands (E).*

From a second fat quarter:

Cut 2 rectangles, 6½" × 14½", for the center section (B).

From *each* of 2 different fat quarters:

Cut 2 rectangles, 7" × 14½", for the side panels C-1 and C-2 (4 total).

Cut 2 squares, 3½" × 3½", for the pocket flaps (4 total).

From a fifth fat quarter:

Cut 2 rectangles, 6½" × 16½", for the pocket (D).***

From the sixth fat quarter:

Cut 4 strips, 3¾" × 20", for the handles (F).

From the assorted leftover fat-quarter scraps:

Cut a total of 20 squares, 3½" × 3½", for the prairie points.

From the lining fabric:

Cut 1 rectangle, 19½" × 43".

From the thin batting or diaper flannel:

Cut 1 rectangle, 19½" × 43".

Cut 2 strips, 1½" × 38", for the handles.

From the iron-on stabilizer:

Cut 4 strips, 1½" × 22", for the handles.

* If you prefer, you can cut A and E from different fabrics.

**If you use a directional fabric for A, consider piecing it along the bottom edge so the motif is symmetrical on the front and back of the tote.

*** If you plan to embroider the pockets, position and embroider the design on the pocket fabric before you cut the pocket pieces to their correct dimensions. Fold the layers as in Assembling the Tote, Step 1, place a piece of batting between the folded layers, and stipple stitch around the embroidery. Trim each pocket to measure 6½" × 8¼", and proceed with the project instructions.

Made by Cheryl Gilman, 2007.

Assembling the Outer Bag

Use a ¼" seam allowance for all seams unless noted otherwise.

1. Fold each pocket rectangle (D) in half crosswise, wrong sides together, to measure 6½" × 8¼". With right sides together and raw edges aligned, place a folded pocket piece at 1 end of each center strip (B). Baste the pockets to the center strips along the sides. Make 2.

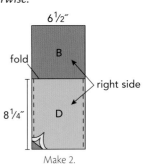

Make 2.

2. With right sides together and long raw edges aligned, stitch side panels (C-1 and C-2) to opposite sides of each center unit from Step 1. Press and topstitch next to seamlines, as desired. Make 2 identical panels.

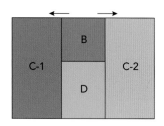

Make 2.

3. For the prairie points, fold each 3½″ assorted fat-quarter square in half diagonally. Press. Fold the triangle in half diagonally again, matching the raw edges. Press. Make 20.

Make 20.

4. With raw edges aligned, place 7 prairie points along the top edge and 3 prairie points along the bottom edge of each panel from Step 2 as shown. Overlap the prairie points by approximately ¾″, and then pin and baste them along the raw edges.

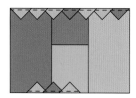

5. Arrange the units from Step 4, the 2 upper-band strips (E), and the

bottom piece (A) as shown. Sew the units, strips, and bottom piece together. Press the seams open. Topstitch the seams along the upper bands (E) by sewing on the upper band side.

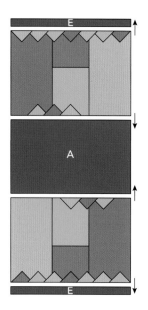

Making and Adding the Handles

1. Refer to Handle Ideas and How-Tos (page 51). Each handle for the basic tote is made using the Folded and Stitched handle method (page 55), with 2 strips 3¾″ × 20″ (F), 2 strips of iron-on stabilizer 1½″ × 22″, and 1 or 2 strips of batting or diaper flannel 1½″ × 38″. Position ends of stabilizer strips away from fabric seamlines. Trim to fit as necessary.

2. Trim each handle strip to measure 28″ to 36″, as desired, and embellish with decorative stitching.

3. Place 1 handle strip at each end of the outer bag, as desired, extending the handle ends 1¼″ above the tote's edges as shown. Baste the handles in place.

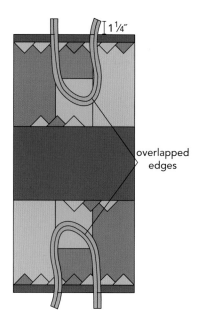

overlapped edges

Finishing the Tote

1. Place the tote body and the 19½″ × 43″ rectangle of lining fabric right sides together. Place the 19½″ × 43″ piece of batting or diaper flannel on top of the lining. Smooth the layers, pin them together along the band strips (E), and stitch along the top and bottom edges.

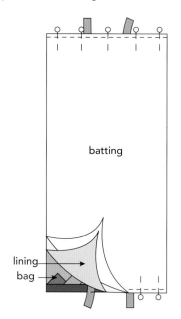

batting

lining

bag

2. Turn the bag to the right side. Press. Topstitch along the top edge of the band strips (E). Pin the layers together along the tote's long edges and baste.

Quilting Suggestion

Serpentine stitch 2 rows through the band strips (E). Repeat the same stitch along the length of the bag, approximately every 1½″. Lift each prairie point along the upper edge of the bag, and begin stitching at the band. As you approach a prairie point along the bottom edge, reduce your stitch length and stitch in place a few times. Raise the needle and lift the presser foot, fold the prairie point up and move to a stitch location as close to the folded prairie point as possible. Lower the presser foot, resume sewing after stitching in place a few times, and continue with the stitch pattern. Trim long threads.

the corners, press, and topstitch around the edges.

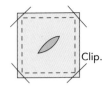

Clip.

Make 2.

6. Press each pocket flap from Step 5 in half diagonally with the flap-front fabric facing outward. Place a folded and pressed flap over each pocket, and stitch a button in place through all the layers to secure.

7. Cut a 10″ length from each package of embroidery floss. Refer to Tassels (pages 61–62), and use each package of embroidery floss to make a tassel. Using a 10″ length of floss, make a loop through the top of each tassel. Wrap the loop around each button several times to secure.

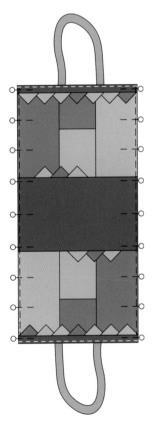

4. If necessary, trim the long edges of the tote to straighten the rectangle. Fold the tote in half with the lining side out and raw side edges aligned. Tuck the bottom of the bag 2½″ to the inside, and pin the layers together. Stitch ½″ and then ¼″ from the raw edges. Serge the raw edges, or finish with a zigzag stitch.

right side of lining

Tuck up 2½″.

3. Stitch in the ditch along the vertical and horizontal seams, stitching across the top of the prairie points in the horizontal seams; then machine quilt as desired.

5. Pin 2 different 3½″ pocket flap squares right sides together, stitch around the perimeter ¼″ from the raw edges, and clip the corners. Make a 1½″-long diagonal cut in the backing square, being careful not to cut through to the flap front. Turn the flap right side out, smooth and shape

Make It "More So!"

- Embellish the pocket fabric before you cut and assemble the pocket pieces (D).

- Stitch buttons on the prairie points along the bottom edge of the bag.

- Couch coordinating decorative threads onto the bag when you are machine quilting to add textural interest.

- Stitch flat lace to the sides of each pocket piece (D) when you baste the pocket to the bag. After the panels are attached, fold the lace over the new seams and stitch in place. If the lace is finished on both edges, simply place it over the seams and stitch.

Made by Susie Kincy, 2007.

Made by Annette Barca, 2007.

Made by Carla Zimmermann, 2007.

Made by Anastasia Riordan, 2007.

Made by Barbara Dau, 2007.

Made by Lucia Pan, 2007.

Fat-Quarter Carryall

FINISHED SIZE: approximately 18½" × 16¼"
(plus the gusset)

This breezy tote—a showcase for six coordinating fat quarters—is destined to become a classic. No doubt you'll find a hundred different ways to put it to use. It offers lots of room for fantastic embellishment and is easy enough to make that you'll want to make more than one. Imagine, for example, this pretty, practical bag made up in fabrics to match each season . . . or done in child-friendly prints for overnighters at Grandma's house. My new *Spring Bouquet* fabric and embroidery is perfect for a seasonal carryall; it includes large and small-scale flowers, stripes, medium-value flowers, and dark leaves to showcase the embroidery. While my *Kimono Art* fabric and embroideries have an Asian feel, the bag works year round.

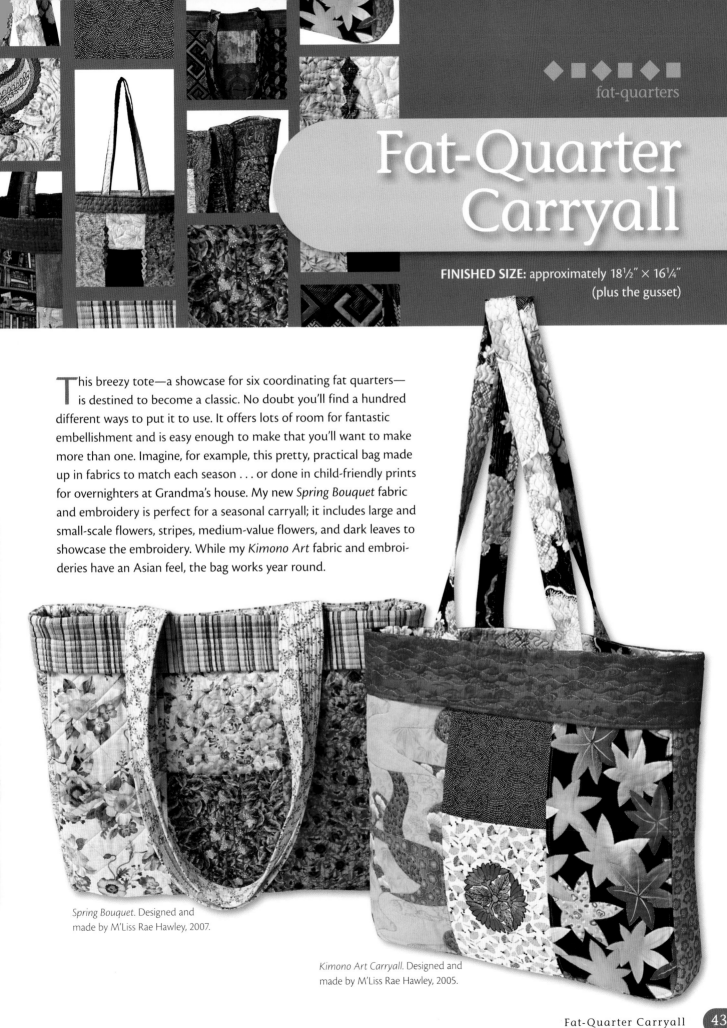

Spring Bouquet. Designed and made by M'Liss Rae Hawley, 2007.

Kimono Art Carryall. Designed and made by M'Liss Rae Hawley, 2005.

Materials for the Basic Bag

Unless noted otherwise, yardages are based on fabric that measures 42" wide after laundering.

A fat quarter assumes fabric that measures 17½" × 20" after laundering.

Bag body and handle: 6 assorted fat quarters

Lining: 1⅛ yards

Crib-size batting: 45" × 60"

Medium to heavyweight iron-on stabilizer: ⅛ yard (40" wide)

Matching and/or contrasting threads for topstitching and/or quilting

Decorative thread for handle (optional)

Cutting

Cut measurements include ¼"-wide seam allowances.

From 1 fat quarter:

Cut 2 pieces, 6½" × 17", for the pockets (A).*

From a second fat quarter:

Cut 2 pieces, 6½" × 17", for the center panel (B).

From *each* of 2 different fat quarters:

Cut 2 pieces, 7" × 17", for the side panels (C-1 and C-2) (4 total).

From a fifth fat quarter:

Cut 3 strips, 4" × 18", for the gusset (D).

From the sixth fat quarter:

Cut 3 strips, 6½" × 18", for the top band (E).

From the lining fabric:

Cut 2 pieces, 21" × 19", for the front and back panels.

Cut 3 strips, 4" × 18", for the gusset.

Cut 2 strips, 3¾" × 40", for the handles.

From the batting:

Cut 1 strip, 2¾" × 54", for the top band.

Cut 1 strip, 3¾" × 54", for the gusset.

Cut 2 pieces, 8" × 9", for the pockets.*

Cut 2 pieces, 21" × 19", for the front and back panels.

Cut 4 strips, 1⅜" × 40", for the handles.

From the iron-on stabilizer:

Cut 2 strips, 1⅜" × 40", for the handles.

* If you plan to embroider the pockets, position and embroider the design on the pocket fabric before you cut the pocket pieces to their correct dimensions. Fold the layers as in Assembling the Tote, Step 1, place a piece of batting between the folded layers, and stipple stitch around the embroidery. Trim each pocket to 6½" × 8½", and proceed with the project instructions.

Assembling the Tote

Use a ¼" seam allowance for all seams.

1. Fold each pocket piece (A) in half, wrong sides together, across the width to make a 6½" × 8½" piece (see * following Cutting, left). With right sides up and raw edges aligned, place a folded pocket piece at 1 end of each center panel (B). Baste the pockets to the center panels along the sides.

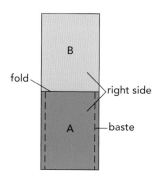

2. With rights sides together and long raw edges aligned, stitch side panels (C-1 and C-2) to opposite sides of each center unit from Step 1 as shown. Press. Make 2 identical panels.

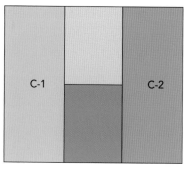

Make 2.

Made by John James, 2007.

3. Layer a 21″ × 19″ lining piece wrong side up, a 21″ × 19″ piece of batting, and a unit from Step 2 right side up. Smooth the layers; baste. Quilt in the ditch along the seams on both sides of the pocket. Add additional quilting as desired. Trim the edges of the batting and lining even with the raw edges of the panel.

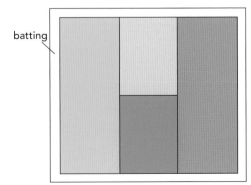

batting

Make 2.

4. Use the pattern on page 46 to make a curved template. Use the template to trim gentle curves around the bottom corners of both panels from Step 3.

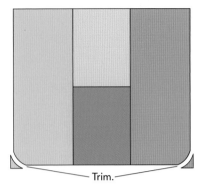

Trim.

5. Stitch the 3 strips of gusset fabric (D) together end to end. Press the seams in one direction. Stitch the three 4″ × 18″ strips of lining fabric together end to end. Press the seams in one direction. Lay the pieced lining strip wrong side up. Center the 3¾″ × 54″ piece of batting on top of the lining, and the pieced gusset strip right side up on top of the batting. Smooth the layers; baste. Quilt as desired, and then trim the edges of the batting even with the fabric.

6. Stitch the 3 top band strips (E) together end to end. Press the seams in one direction. Fold the strip in half lengthwise, wrong sides together, and press. Insert the 2¾″ × 54″ strip of batting inside the fold, and smooth the layers; baste. Quilt as desired, and then trim the ends of the batting even with the band.

fold

Trim.

Making and Adding the Handles

1. Refer to Handle Ideas and How-Tos (page 51). Each handle for the basic tote is made using the Folded and Stitched handle method (page 55), with 1 strip of lining/handle fabric 3¾″ × 40″, 1 strip of iron-on stabilizer 1⅜″ × 40″, and the 2 strips of batting or diaper flannel 1½″ × 40″.

2. Trim each handle strip to measure 28″ to 36″, as desired, and embellish with decorative stitching.

Finishing the Tote

1. Place the gusset and the front panel wrong sides together, centering the gusset seams so they fall on or near the bottom (curved) corners of the panel. Pin generously, and sew the gusset to the panel with a scant ¼" seam. Trim the excess gusset tails.

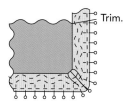

Trim.

Curves Ahead!

Sew with the gusset on top so you can see around the curves as you come to them.

---

2. Turn the panel and gusset right sides together and re-stitch, this time taking a full ¼" seam allowance to catch all the layers and to make a French seam.

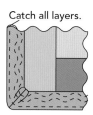

Catch all layers.

3. Turn the unit right side out, and topstitch the seams on the front panel, including all around the outer curved edge.

4. Repeat Steps 1–3 to sew the back panel to the gusset.

Cheryl Gilman used folded fabric elements, which she embellished with beads, to add interest and texture to her tote.

5. Turn the tote inside out and use the center panel seams as a guide to position and baste both ends of 1 handle to the front panel. Allow the handle ends to extend approximately 1½" above the upper edge of the panel. Repeat to baste a handle to the wrong side of the back panel.

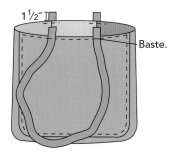

1½"

Baste.

6. Measure the circumference of the bag opening, and trim the top band to this measurement plus ½". Fold the band in half, and sew the short ends together.

fold

7. With the tote still inside out, align the long raw edge of the band from Step 6 right sides together with the top raw edge of the tote. Position the band so the seam aligns with the gusset seam. Stitch the band to the tote. Turn the tote right side out, turn the band to the right side, and topstitch.

Make It Stable!

Stitch the ends of the handles down through all the layers of the tote for added stability.

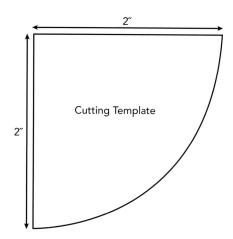

2"

2"

Cutting Template

Made by Cheryl Gilman, 2007.

Made by Lucia Pan, 2007.

Made by Susie Kincy, 2007.

Cosmetic Bag

FINISHED SIZE: approximately 11½″ × 8″

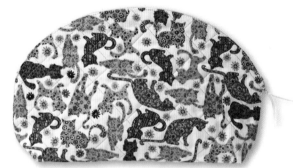

Here's a little something just the right size to tuck in your purse or carry-on for your next long flight. It takes just two fat quarters of fabric: one for the bag and one for the lining. You can also save a few steps—and some fabric—by making your bag from prequilted fabric. In that case there's no need to purchase lining fabric, and the outer-bag fabric is already layered and quilted.

Calico Sisters. Designed and made by M'Liss Rae Hawley, 2007.

Night Flight to Buenos Aires. Designed and made by M'Liss Rae Hawley, 2007.

Materials for the Basic Bag

A fat quarter assumes fabric that measures 17½" × 20" after laundering.

Outer bag: 1 fat quarter

Lining: 1 fat quarter

Thin batting or diaper flannel: 18" × 20" piece

Matching and/or contrasting threads for topstitching and/or quilting

Zipper: 14"

Assembling the Bag

Use a ¼" seam allowance for all seams.

1. Layer the fat quarter of lining fabric, wrong side up, the batting or diaper flannel, and the fat quarter of outer-bag fabric, right side up, to make a miniature quilt sandwich; pin or baste.

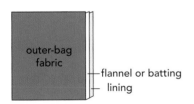

2. Quilt and/or embellish as desired. See Embellishment Options and Fantastic Finishes (page 57) for embellishing ideas.

3. Use the pattern on page 50 to cut the body of the bag from the quilted, embellished fabric. Mark the large circles on the curved edges of the fabric with a fabric marker or pins. Serge or finish the raw edges with a zigzag stitch.

4. Using the marks or pins you placed in Step 3 as a guide for the ends of the zipper, align 1 edge of the zipper right sides together with 1 curved edge of the bag. Open the zipper and, with the zipper side up, use a zipper foot to sew the zipper to the bag. Close the zipper, and repeat to sew the other edge of the zipper to the opposite curved edge of the bag.

5. Fold the bag in half with the lining side out, bringing the curved edges together. Open the zipper and stitch the side seams.

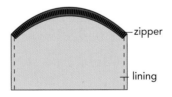

6. Fold the bag—still lining side out—so 1 side seam runs down the center, facing you. Measure 1½" from the tip; mark, and stitch across the point to form a gusset. Repeat on the other side seam. Trim the excess

fabric, leaving a ¼" seam allowance, and serge or finish the seam with a zigzag stitch.

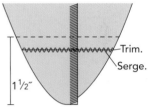

7. Turn the bag right side out, and press. If you'd like, add a decorative doodad to the zipper pull.

It's So Simple!

Create a pull tab by threading a 5" piece of ¼" silk cording, leather, or other decorative embellishment through the zipper pull and knotting it off. If necessary, trim the ends at a diagonal to prevent raveling.

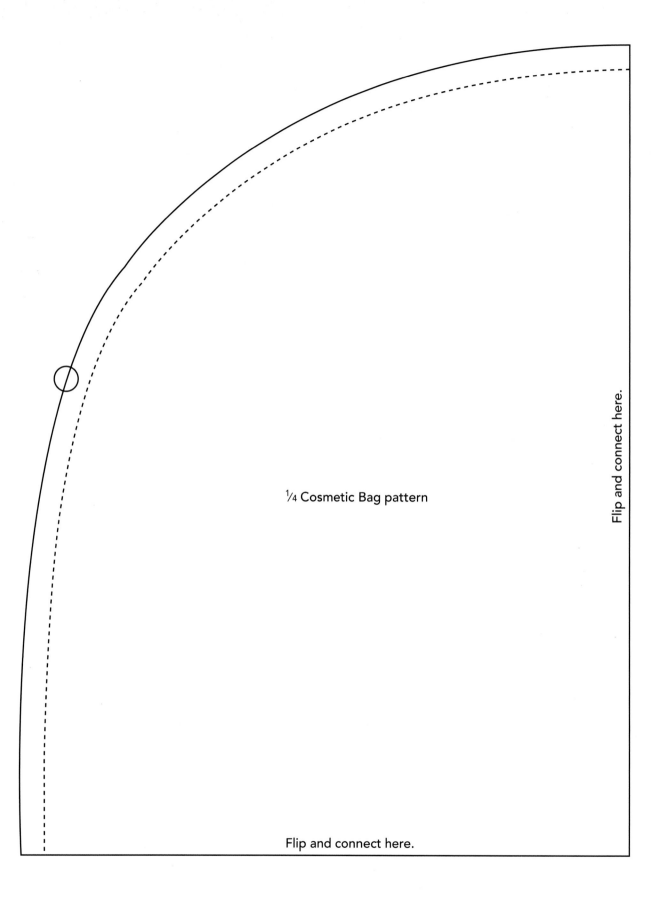

¼ Cosmetic Bag pattern

Flip and connect here.

Flip and connect here.

Handle Ideas and How-Tos

With the exception of the Small Shoulder Purse with Flap (page 6) and the Cosmetic Bag (page 48), the instructions for each basic bag include a suggested handle treatment. That doesn't mean you must limit yourself to that option. If you study the photos scattered throughout the book, you'll discover that there are many, many alternatives. In this chapter, you'll find close-up photographs of some of these options, as well as the how-tos for making some handles of your own.

Using Purchased Handles

There are loads of ready-made handle options available at craft and sewing stores. You can even *recycle* handles from purses and totes you find at thrift shops, flea markets, garage sales . . . and in the back of your closet. Here are just a few ideas.

Beaded Handles

Look for prestrung beads, shells, and trinkets to enhance the color story and/or theme of your bag.

Gilded Age by M'Liss Rae Hawley (page 14): three strands of gold beads braided for an elegant handle treatment.

Small Shoulder Purse with Flap by Susie Kincy (page 10).

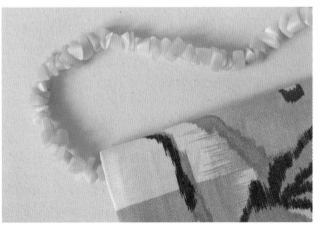

Small Shoulder Purse with Flap by Carla Zimmermann (page 10).

Braided Handles

Purchase prebraided handles, or braid your own from lengths of silk, metallic, or fabric-covered cording; ribbons, decorative yarns, and fibers; twine; thin leather stripping, or strips of fabric. Mix colors, mix fibers. The sky's the limit here!

Petite Textures by M'Liss Rae Hawley (page 9): an example of double-ply strips of leather, purchased in Argentina.

Meow! by M'Liss Rae Hawley (page 10): an example of braided handmade cording.

North by Northwest by M'Liss Rae Hawley (page 31): fabric-covered cording, ruched and braided.

Saddle Bag Purse by Vicki DeGraaf (page 30): braided strips of wool.

Chains

Choose fine or chunky chain—single-strand, twisted, or braided—in gold, silver, or some other metallic finish. Just be sure the scale of the chain is in proper proportion to the size of the purse or tote.

Ribbon Purse by Cheryl Gilman (page 18): Note the hardware used to attach the handle.

Cording, Ribbon, and Trim

Many purses and totes in this book use cording—from the finest gauge to the more substantial home-decorator varieties—ribbon, and other trims for handle material. Here are just a few examples. Study the bags throughout the book for many, many more.

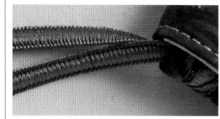

Small Shoulder Purse with Flap by Susie Kincy (page 12): flat silk cord.

Small Shoulder Purse with Flap by Lucia Pan (page 12): twisted decorator cord.

Small Shoulder Purse with Flap by Annette Barca (page 11): ribbon trim.

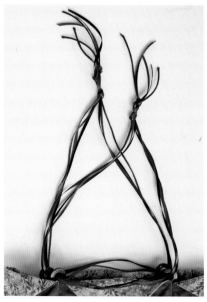

Four Continents by M'Liss Rae Hawley (page 24): bundled and tied silk ribbon and cording.

Leather and Vinyl Handles

These handles lend a traditional touch to your handmade purse or tote.

Twin Dragons by M'Liss Rae Hawley (page 36): I found these beautiful red leather handles while on a trip to France.

M'Liss's Garden by M'Liss Rae Hawley (page 11): another gorgeous red leather handle.

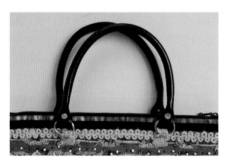

Ribbon Purse by Cheryl Gilman (page 18): These handles are the perfect match in color and style for the more casual torn denim strips, grosgrain ribbon, and sisal trims Cheryl used for her ribbon purse.

Plastic Handles

Plastic handles come in a wide variety of colors, shapes, and styles and make a nice alternative to wood or leather.

Ribbon Purse by Cheryl Gilman (page 18): Could this color be more perfect?

The Cube Purse by John James (page 23): Faux tortoise shell is a good match for the autumn color story of this bag.

Saddle Bag Purse by Carla Zimmermann (page 30): Sleek and simple!

Webbing

You'll find webbing in various colors, weaves, widths, and textures. Use it as it comes, or embellish it with decorative stitching.

Small Shoulder Purse with Flap by Annette Barca (page 11): Simple black webbing complements this purse's holiday theme.

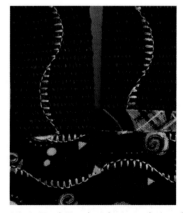

Mix & Match Tote by John James (page 35): Note the decorative stitching added to the purchased webbing.

Odds and Ends

There is no end to the creative solutions you can invent if you just use your imagination.

Zippers by M'Liss Rae Hawley (page 13): Zippers stitched end to end make the perfect handle for this clever purse.

The Cube Purse by Cheryl Gilman (page 20): Large-scale, colorful pompom trim adds to the harlequin effect.

The Cube Purse by Susie Kincy (page 22): Susie covered nice fat cording with fabric from my *Garden Court* fabric line and then attached the handle with coordinated, fabric-covered buttons.

Wood/Bamboo Handles

Use these as they are; wrap them with ribbon, fabric, or suede; or paint or stain them to match the bag. Attach them with rings, tabs, or other fasteners.

The Cube by M'Liss Rae Hawley (page 19): I love the detailing on this wooden handle.

Mix & Match Tote by Susie Kincy (page 35): Delicate bamboo handles add additional texture to the large-scale print and colorful embroideries from my *Kimono Art II* fabric and embroidery collections.

Saddle Bag Purse by Lucia Pan (page 29): The shape of the handle takes this purse to a whole new level.

Do-It-Yourself Handles

Here are step-by-step instructions for a few handle options—two more "sedate"—and one not!

Folded and Stitched

Experience the World with M'Liss by M'Liss Rae Hawley (page 38).

This is a simple, versatile handle that works well for many purses and totes. It is the handle given in the basic bag instructions for the Fat-Quarter Tote Bag (page 38) and for the Fat-Quarter Carryall (page 43); the instructions for each project tell you what materials you need and how to cut them. You can adapt this handle for other purses and totes; just be certain to keep the handle in proportion (length and width) to the size of the bag.

1. If required, place strips of handle fabric for each handle right sides together at right angles and stitch them together with a diagonal seam. Trim the seam allowance to ¼" and press the seam open.

Stitch.

2. If the instructions call for interfacing, center a strip of interfacing, adhesive side down, on the wrong side of each handle strip, butting the strips if necessary to cover the length. Fuse following the manufacturer's instructions. Trim as necessary.

3. Center the strip (or strips) of batting over the handle unit, and fold the long raw edges of the handle fabric over the interfacing (if applicable) and batting, overlapping them as shown. Press, and then baste down the center of the strip.

4. Use matching, contrasting, or decorative threads to quilt or embellish each handle with decorative stitching. **Note:** Be sure to remove the basting stitch.

5. Attach the handles to the bag as instructed.

Thread-Covered Cording

Small Shoulder Purse with Flap by Carla Zimmermann (page 10).

Here's a simple technique that will give even the plainest purchased cording a designer touch.

Note: You may need to lower the feed dogs on your machine for this technique. Experiment on a scrap of cording before you begin.

1. Outfit your sewing machine with a cording, braiding, or appliqué foot, and thread the machine with the same thread in the top and in the bobbin. Place a piece of narrow nylon or string cording under the foot, leaving a 2″–3″ tail behind the foot to hold on to. Set the machine to a zigzag or satin stitch, making sure the stitch is wide enough to cover the width of the cord. Stitch down the length of cord.

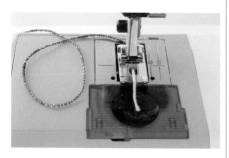

2. If necessary for coverage, or if desired for effect, stitch over the cording again, using the same or different-colored thread, depending upon the effect you wish to achieve.

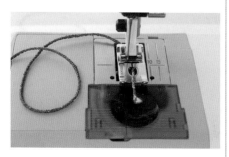

3. When you are satisfied with the coverage, change the top and bobbin threads to a decorative thread (e.g., rayon or metallic), increase the stitch length, and complete another round of stitching.

The results can be stunning—and widely varied—depending upon the thickness of the cording, the types and colors of thread, and the stitch width you use. The covered cords can be used singly or in multiples: twisted, braided, or knotted.

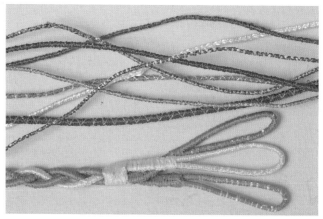

Filled Plastic Tubing

Ribbon Purse by Susie Kincy (page 17).

Susie Kincy used aquarium tubing (found at a pet store) and filled it with colorful seed beads to make a unique handle for her ribbon purse. She attached it to the bag in the seam she stitched to insert the zipper. Here are her tips on selecting and working with tubing.

- Make sure the tubing is large enough in diameter to accommodate the intended contents, yet not so large that it won't fit under the presser foot on your machine.

- Crimp the tubing with your fingers to make sure it is pliable enough to work with.

- If you are stuffing it with something loose, such as beads, sew 1 end shut before you start filling the tubing. A small funnel is helpful!

- Shake the tubing or thump it with your finger to make sure the contents settle.

- When attaching the handle to the bag, sew back and forth only enough to secure the tubing. If you overdo it, you will eventually cut off the plastic, especially if the tubing is narrow.

Embellishment Options and Fantastic Finishes

This chapter abounds in ideas and tips for enlivening your purses and totes with embellishments and gives you some useful—and creative—information for bringing your project to a perfect conclusion.

Embellishment: Making It Yours

The purses and totes pictured in this book are filled with inspiration for fantastic embellishment. You can barely turn a page without discovering another way to enrich your creation. Many of these ideas are detailed here, but I couldn't possibly cover them all, so keep your eyes open as you view the individual project chapters.

Appliqués

Hello Kitty for Adrienne by M'Liss Rae Hawley (page 12): I found the Hello Kitty fabric while shopping in San Francisco when I was pregnant with my daughter, Adrienne . . . over 23 years ago! The lace is from a prom dress I made for myself while in high school.

If you can get a needle through it, you can probably stitch it to your purse or tote. Consider fabric motifs, embroideries, lace, clothing labels, coated paper . . . you get the idea!

Beads/Crystals

Gold by M'Liss Rae Hawley (page 13): I used gold silk dupioni and embroidered a cherry blossom in gold metallic thread (from my *Kimono Art* collection), then hand beaded it with gold crystals and beads. The purse coordinates with a gown I made for a special event.

Cluster them, sprinkle them, or use them as edgings, fringes, and trims. Larger ones make excellent closures and zipper pulls.

> **Tip**
> When topstitching next to beads, use the zipper foot!

Buttons

Mardi Gras by M'Liss Rae Hawley (page 11):
Sometimes less is better! I planned to use many
gold buttons, then "reduced my variables" to one
special button that continues the theme, shape,
and colors of the purse.

From the everyday ivory shirt variety to
one-of-a-kind hand-painted works of art,
buttons make fabulous embellishments.
For added color and texture, tie them
on with embroidery floss or narrow
ribbon, or anchor them with beads.

Couching

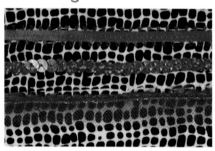

Along the Andes by M'Liss Rae Hawley (page 27):
I couched sequin trim; silk, organza, and grosgrain
ribbons; tiny tasseled trim; metallic thread; and
other red "goodies"—all with red thread—to make
a strong statement on my black-and-white saddle
bag purse.

Layer ribbons, yarns, threads, tassels,
strips of fabric and tulle (flat, twisted,
or braided), cording, rickrack, lace, and
other decorative trims over the fabric
or quilted surface of your purse or tote,
using a zigzag, serpentine, or other decorative stitch and the appropriate foot
attachment. Use thread that matches
the color of the trim, or a different
color or texture (e.g., metallic thread)
for contrast. You can even leave the
ends to dangle free.

Collage/Confetti

Garden Court Winery by M'Liss Rae Hawley
(page 38): I captured bits and pieces of
colorful fabric with thread to embellish the
handle of my fat-quarter tote.

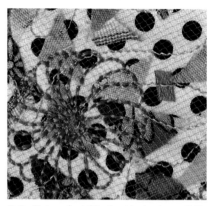

Petite Textures by M'Liss Rae Hawley (page 9): Bits
of fabric and ribbon create confetti! I covered the
flap with tulle and used an allover stipple stitch
and gold metallic thread. The top layer is made
from small motifs placed and embroidered ran-
domly to add more texture, interest, and fun.

Layer scraps and strips of fabric and snippets of thread with organza, netting, or even vinyl, and secure them with lots of free-motion stitchery.

Felting

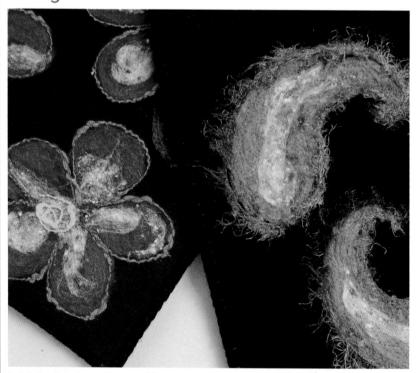

Saddle Bag Purse by Vicki DeGraaf (page 30): Vicki constructed her purse and embellished it with
two different motifs so that it is completely reversible.

Felting adds texture and weight to a purse or tote and is the perfect
technique for a winter accessory.

Decorative Stitching

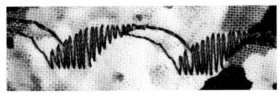

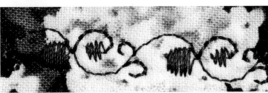

Night Flight to Buenos Aires by M'Liss Rae Hawley (page 48): Decorative stitching is an appealing replacement for the more expected crosshatching on my little cosmetic bag.

Consider the body—and even the handle—of your purse or tote as a canvas for the decorative stitches your sewing machine has to offer. Try silk, rayon, variegated, and metallic threads. For maximum impact, choose a thread color that contrasts with the background fabric.

Crazy Patch

Small Shoulder Purse with Flap by Vicki DeGraaf (page 11): Vicki used old silk ties for the crazy-patch flap on her small shoulder purse. The result is pure Victoriana.

Assemble your treasured scraps of silk, velvet, and lace on a lightweight foundation to create fabric for your purse or tote. If you wish, embellish with beads and/or decorative stitches.

Ribbon Work/Weaving

Wedding Memories by M'Liss Rae Hawley (page 10): I hand basted ribbons and trims onto the purse flap, then secured them with machine stitching. I also collected mother-of-pearl buttons, wedding-dress-type trim, and a string of pearls for the handle to complete the embellishments.

Photo Transfer

M'Liss's Garden by M'liss Rae Hawley (page 11): I used a favorite photo Michael took of a sunflower in our yard and transferred it onto fabric. The bag fabric is from my Jo-Ann line, *M'Liss's Garden*. Notice the seed beads embellishing the flower centers. A bejeweled frog lies nearby.

Small Shoulder Purse with Flap by Peggy Johnson (page 12): Peggy enlarged the basic small shoulder purse slightly to accommodate two favorite photographs of her granddaughter and the family dachshunds.

Transfer favorite photos to fabric to incorporate them into your purses and totes. Photo transfers are great for personalizing labels too.

Machine Embroidery

Small Shoulder Purse with Flap by Susie Kincy (page 10): Susie used an embroidered motif from my *Quilting with M'Liss* collection to embellish the flap of her small shoulder purse.

There are countless ways to incorporate machine embroidery into your purses and totes, and you'll see many examples throughout this book. See Tips for Machine Embroidery (right), and refer to page 63 for information on the featured embroidery collections.

Pin Tucks

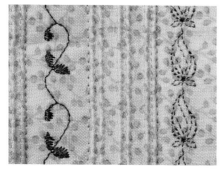

The Cube Purse by Susie Kincy (page 22): Susie used contrasting thread and decorative stitching to highlight the pin tucks on this charming purse.

Pin tucks add texture to the surface of your purse or tote. For further interest, embellish the pin-tucked areas with beads, trims, and decorative stitching.

Tips for Machine Embroidery

- Prewash the fabric you plan to use as background for the embroidery designs. Washing will preshrink the fabric, which is a necessary step.

- Begin your embroidery with a new needle and change it during the process if the point becomes dull. Skipped stitches are one indication of a dull needle. Some embroidery designs have more than 10,000 stitches. A dull needle can distort the design.

- Outfit your machine with an embroidery foot.

- Prewind several bobbins with polyester, rayon, or cotton bobbin-fill thread. Or purchase prewound bobbins such as those manufactured by Robison-Anton. Choose white or black, using the background fabric as your guide; or you may want to change the bobbin thread as the color of the top thread changes.

- Select a fabric stabilizer to use under the background fabric. There are many types of stabilizers available—my favorite is a midweight tear-away product manufactured by Sulky (see Resources on page 63). Whichever you choose, read the manufacturer's instructions *carefully*. Some stabilizers are heat- or water-sensitive. I prefer a tear-away stabilizer when I machine embroider on 100% cotton fabric. If the fabric is prone to puckering, try a water-soluble or heat-sensitive stabilizer. Stitch a sample to test.

- An embroidery hoop is key; it keeps the fabric from shifting as you embroider the designs. If possible, place the fabric in the hoop so that it is on the straight grain. Avoid puckers and pleats. The fabric should be pulled taut but not too tight.

- Stitch a test of the desired embroidery design, using the fabric, threads, and stabilizer you plan to use for the project. You'll be able to tell whether the thread tension is correct, whether the thread coverage is sufficient, and whether the embroidered design will look good on the background fabric you've chosen so you can make any necessary adjustments. If you wish, you can incorporate your test design into your label or quilt backing.

Finishing Touches

Finishing details mean a lot, so be sure to give them the same attention you've given to every other element of your purse or tote.

Closures

There are lots of ways to add closures to your purses and totes. Zippers are the most common and utilitarian, and are noted in the basic bag instructions for the Ribbon Purse (page 14) and the Cosmetic Bag (page 48). You can add them to many of the other purses and totes as well. However, don't overlook buttons, ties, snaps, hooks, hook-and-loop tape, and other options.

Small Shoulder Purse with Flap by Carla Zimmermann (page 10): Carla found a gorgeous decorative bead for the closure on this beautiful purse.

Small Shoulder Purse with Flap by Barbara Dau (page 10): This marcasite button closure seems made for Barbara's elegant black and silver purse.

Ribbon Purse by Cheryl Gilman (page 18): Dress up a zipper with a decorative pull, as Cheryl has done with this "spicy" embellishment.

Binding

The directions for the Saddle Bag Purse (page 27) instruct you to finish the edges of the purse with binding and tell you what fabric you need and how to cut it. However, there may be other occasions when you want to use binding—for example, to finish an inside seam. I always use the same method (see my *Round Robin Renaissance* book for those instructions, pages 72–74).

Note: Cut strips in a width that is proportional to the size of the bag. Note that you will be folding the strip in half lengthwise and taking in ½" in seam allowances. If the edges of the bag are straight, cut the strips on the straight grain of the fabric. If the edges are curved, cut the strips on the bias of the fabric.

Tassels

Tassels can be whimsical, ethnic, elegant, or funky, depending upon what they are made of (e.g., silk, yarn, floss, ribbon, or beads) and where you place them on your bag.

Saddle Bag Purse by Annette Barca (page 30): Silky gold tassels lend an exotic finish to Annette's richly hued purse.

You can purchase your tassels ready made or make your own. It's easy!

1. Remove the wrapper from the skein of embroidery floss and fold the floss in half as shown. Trim two 8" lengths of floss from one loose end, and tie one length tightly around the skein fold with a double square knot.

2. Wrap the second length of floss tightly around the doubled skein, approximately ½" from the bound fold you made in Step 1. Knot the ends, thread the tails onto a large-eyed needle, and bury them in the center of the tassel.

3. Using sharp scissors, cut through the looped floss at the opposite end of the tassel so the ends are even. Fluff the floss, and the tassel is ready to attach.

The Grand Finale

If your bag warrants it, consider adding a decorative pin or brooch.

Small Shoulder Purse with Flap by Carla Zimmermann (page 13): Carla added an appropriately scaled gold brooch to the asymmetrical flap—a nice counterpoint to the straight lines and angles of her purse.

Fat-Quarter Tote Bag by Carla Zimmermann (page 42): A diamond-shaped brooch nicely balances the Western-themed fabrics in Carla's tote.

And finally, don't forget to add a label to the lining of your bag!

Detail of label in my *Four Continents Origami Bag* (page 24).

Detail of label in my *Meow!* bag (page 10).

Resources

For quilting supplies, including fast2fuse interfacing:

Cotton Patch
1025 Brown Ave.
Lafayette, CA 94549
(800) 835-4418 or
(925) 283-7883
Email: CottonPa@aol.com
Website: www.quiltusa.com

Island Fabrics Etc.
Freeland, WA
(360) 331-4435
www.islandfabrics.com

Note: Fabric manufacturers discontinue fabrics regularly. Exact fabrics shown may no longer be available.

For information about trims:

M&J Trimming
1010 Sixth Avenue
New York, NY 10018
(212) 704-8019
www.mjtrim.com

For information about thread:

Robison-Anton Textile Company
www.robison-anton.com

For information about Sulky products:

Sulky of America
www.sulky.com

To locate your nearest Husqvarna Viking dealer:

Husqvarna Viking
www.husqvarnaviking.com

Concord Sewing Center
2958 Treat Boulevard #A
Concord, CA 94518
(925) 825-2122
www.concordsewingcenter.com

For information about M'Liss's fabric:

Jo-Ann Fabric and Craft Stores
www.joann.com

For information about M'Liss's Quilters & Crafters Value Kit and other OLFA products:

Available at your local Jo-Ann Fabric and Craft Stores or www.olfa.com

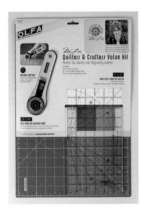

Embroidery Collections

Kimono Art, by M'Liss Rae Hawley, Disk Part # 756 259800, Inspira collection, multiformat CD-ROM

Kimono Art II, by M'Liss Rae Hawley, Disk Part #620 037296, Inspira collection, multiformat CD-ROM

My Favorite Quilt Designs, by M'Liss Rae Hawley, Disk Part #756 253300, Inspira collection, multiformat CD-ROM

Spring View, by M'Liss Rae Hawley, Disk Part #756 255100, Inspira collection, multiformat CD-ROM

Textures & Techniques with M'Liss, by M'Liss Rae Hawley, Husqvarna Viking Embroidery 181

Quilting with M'Liss, by M'Liss Rae Hawley, Husqvarna Viking Embroidery 175

Delicate and Dainty, Viking #65

Seaside, EZ Sew Designs, part #756 103400

About the Author

M'Liss Rae Hawley is an accomplished quilting teacher, lecturer, and embroidery and textile designer. She conducts workshops and seminars throughout the world and likes to break quilting down to the basics to show students that it can be easy and fun at any skill level.

As the best-selling author of ten books, including *Phenomenal Fat Quarter Quilts* (2004), *Get Creative! with M'Liss Rae Hawley* (2005), *M'Liss Rae Hawley's Round Robin Renaissance* (2006), *Mariner's Medallion Quilts* (2006), *M'Liss Rae Hawley's Fat Quarter Quilts* (2007), *Make Your First Quilt with M'Liss Rae Hawley* (2007), and *M'Liss Rae Hawley's Scrappy Quilts* (2008), and the originator of numerous innovative designs, M'Liss is constantly seeking new boundaries to challenge her students while imparting her enthusiasm and love for the art of quilting.

Although her new PBS television series, *Experience Quilting with M'Liss Rae Hawley*, is in production, M'Liss still finds time to design fabric exclusively for Jo-Ann Fabric and Craft Stores and to be the quilting spokesperson for Husqvarna Viking and Robison-Anton Textile Company.

M'Liss and her husband, Michael, live on Whidbey Island, Washington, in a filbert orchard. Michael is also a best-selling author, a college professor, and the recently retired sheriff of Island County. Their son, Alexander, is a sergeant in the Marine Corps, and their daughter, Adrienne, a recent graduate of Seattle University, is serving in AmeriCorps. Michael and M'Liss share their home with seven dachshunds and four cats.

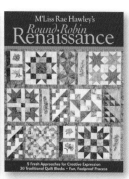
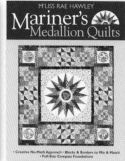